THE KING
AND HIS KINGDOM

JESUS IN THE GOSPEL OF MATTHEW

MIKE MAZZALONGO

BibleTalk.tv

Copyright © 2015 by Mike Mazzalongo

ISBN: 978-0692439531

BibleTalk Books
14998 E. Reno
Choctaw, Oklahoma 73020

Scripture quotations taken from the New American Standard Bible®, Copyright © 1960, 1962, 1963, 1968, 1971, 1972, 1973, 1975, 1977, 1995 by The Lockman Foundation Used by permission. (www.Lockman.org)

TABLE OF CONTENTS

1. THE KING'S BIRTH	5
2. THE KING'S TEMPTATION	15
3. THE KINGDOM CHARACTER	27
4. THE KING IN ACTION	41
5. THE KINGDOM IN CONFLICT	55
6. THE KINGDOM GROWS	69
7. KINGDOM KINDNESS	79
8. WHO IS THE KING?	93
9. THE KINGDOM'S LOSS	109
10. THE KING'S HOUSE	119
11. THE KING'S JUDGEMENT	133
12. THE KING'S VICTORY	147

CHAPTER 1
THE KING'S BIRTH

MATTHEW 1:1-2:23

Each of the four men who recorded the life and ministry of Jesus Christ had his own perspective and background which in turn influenced his writing. These men were contemporaries and witnessed the same events but because of the audience they were writing for their accounts emphasized different (not contradicting) details.

For example, Matthew's gospel describes Jesus as a royal figure, the king of the Jews or the king of heaven. Mark, on the other hand, describes Jesus as the powerful Son of God. He focuses a lot of attention on Jesus' miracles. Luke, the historian, is interested in showing Jesus as fully human. He demonstrates that even though Jesus was the Divine Son of God, He was no less human and experienced a very human life. John's gospel is the most philosophical of the four accounts. He uses imagery (Jesus is light) to convey the concept that Jesus was the embodiment of God's truth.

The purpose of this book will be to follow Matthew's gospel in tracing out Jesus' life, death and resurrection as the King of heaven and earth. We understand that Jesus is at once all of these things (King, Son of God, Son of Man, Truth, etc.), however we will study one of these strands in order to have a greater understanding of the whole.

> Now after Jesus was born in Bethlehem of Judea in the days of Herod the king, magi from the east arrived in Jerusalem, saying, "Where is He who has been born King of the Jews? For we saw His star in the east and have come to worship Him." When Herod the king heard this, he was troubled, and all Jerusalem with him. Gathering together all the chief priests and scribes of the people, he inquired of them where the Messiah was to be born. They said to him, "In Bethlehem of Judea; for this is what has been written by the prophet:
>
> 'And you, Bethlehem, land of Judah,
> Are by no means least among the leaders of Judah;
> For out of you shall come forth a Ruler
> Who will shepherd My people Israel.'"
>
> Then Herod secretly called the magi and determined from them the exact time the star appeared. And he sent them to Bethlehem and said, "Go and search carefully for the Child; and when you have found Him, report to me, so that I too may come and worship Him." After hearing the king, they went their way; and the star, which they had seen in the east, went on before them until it came and stood over the place where the Child was. When they saw the star, they rejoiced exceedingly with great joy. After coming into the house they saw the Child with Mary His mother; and they fell to the ground and worshiped Him. Then, opening their treasures, they

presented to Him gifts of gold, frankincense, and myrrh. And having been warned by God in a dream not to return to Herod, the magi left for their own country by another way.
- Matthew 2:1-12

Although what is discussed here is the birth of Jesus, Matthew provides very little information about the actual birth itself. In chapter one he traces out Jesus' genealogy from Abraham to David down to Joseph his earthly father. He does this to show that Jesus is a direct and true descendant of Abraham; thus, establishing His claim to be the Messiah, since no one who was not a descendant of Abraham specifically through David could claim to be the Messiah according to Scripture.

This being done he moves on to briefly describe Mary's conception by the power of the Holy Spirit, the prophecy of His role as Savior, Joseph's taking her as wife, and a simple declaration of Jesus' subsequent birth. This is all introduced in the first chapter. Matthew saves the details for the characters surrounding Jesus' birth and it is from these that we learn more of His royal nature.

The Wise Men from the East

There are many fables and traditions that have developed about these people. Some say that there were three of them because three gifts were mentioned. We don't actually know the exact number because the Bible doesn't say, however it would be safe to assume there were several since they probably travelled in a caravan in order to cover the great distance through dangerous territory.

What we do know is recorded in the pages of the New Testament. They were from Babylon because this was the only nation that had a serious study of the stars in either astronomy (their position, size, etc.) and astrology (their effect on human affairs). They were Gentiles who knew, somehow, about the hope and promise to the Jews concerning a savior (Messiah). This should not be so surprising since Daniel lived and prophesied concerning the Jewish Messiah while he lived among the Babylonians some 600 years before.

> Then the king promoted Daniel and gave him many great gifts, and he made him ruler over the whole province of Babylon and chief prefect over all the wise men of Babylon.
> - Daniel 2:48

There may have been prophesies given by Daniel but not recorded, yet somehow available to these people for just this occasion.

Matthew describes a "star" that they saw while in their country and then again when they arrived in Judea, which ultimately led them to the baby Jesus. The Bible doesn't tell us how they made the connection between the unusual star they observed in their country and the birth of the Jewish Messiah. The Bible simply states that the star signaled that the Jewish Messiah (promised by the prophets) was born, and based on this they made their way to Jerusalem.

Of course a caravan of high officials (they usually served as advisors to their king or governors) from the east asking questions about the birth of a Jewish king (another title conferred on the Jewish Messiah) was bound to create a stir, and it did. The star they saw was a signal of the birth. They travelled to the most logical place to find a "king" and that was the city of the King and God's temple: Jerusalem.

Their questions draw the interest of the present "king" of the Jewish nation, Herod (we'll have more information on him later) who consults with the priests and teachers about the exact location given by Scripture of the birthplace of the

Messiah. The teachers quote the Old Testament prophet Micah:

> "But as for you, Bethlehem Ephrathah,
> Too little to be among the clans of Judah,
> From you One will go forth for Me to be ruler in Israel.
> His goings forth are from long ago,
> From the days of eternity."
> - Micah 5:2

This prophecy indicated the future birthplace of the Messiah. The way it was quoted suggests that even though Bethlehem was a small place within the land of Judah, it would produce a leader who would not only lead the city or tribe but the entire nation as well. In other words, from Bethlehem would come a king!

The present king, Herod, questions them as to the exact date that they saw the star so as to determine the time frame of the birth. He does this in secret so as to not arouse suspicion and curiosity among the people. Herod pretends to be eager to find this king and sends them away with instructions to report back to him the exact location of the child so he too can worship.

Of course his plan is to get rid of this threat to his power but he can't let them know this. Since he cannot kill them for fear of retaliation by their foreign ruler as well as arousing questions from his own people, he sends them along.

Matthew explains that once they are pointed in the direction of Bethlehem (about two hours south of Jerusalem) they again see the star that guides them to exactly where in the city the child was located. There has been much speculation that this star was really a comet, a shooting or exploding star in order to give a non-miraculous explanation to what these men saw. However, the Bible clearly states that the star was special in a way to distinguish it from the others, and to signal the birth of

Christ at that particular moment in history. The Bible also says that the very same star appeared once again (after their arrival) to lead them to the house where Jesus was.

The timing, the two appearances and its position in the sky (low enough or bright enough to point out a particular house) tell us that this was no comet, no shooting star, but a body of light especially provided by God to lead these men to Christ. If God can send angels to direct the shepherds to Christ, He can as easily provide a star to do the same thing for these Gentiles to find the king they came to see.

They find the child in a house with His mother. Joseph is not mentioned since Mary is the one holding Jesus. Jesus was born in a manger but it seems that at some later time Joseph was able to secure a more permanent place to stay.

The wise men immediately worship the child. They prostrated themselves before Him as was the manner of worship or humbling oneself before God or a ruler. They do not see a child, they correctly (we don't know how) see who and what this child is and is destined to become according to Scripture. What they understood about Him is seen in the gifts they bring:

> **1. Gold** – Gold was not found in Babylon and thus extremely expensive. It was the property of kings, for only they had the resources to obtain it. To offer Him gold was the give Him a gift in keeping with His position. A royal gift for a royal person.
>
> **2. Frankincense** – This substance was a type of sweet incense, very refined, from India. Its main usage was for worship purposes. It was burned as an offering to the gods in religious services. As a child, Jesus had no use for this. It was given to Him as a way of recognizing His divine nature.

3. **Myrrh** – Myrrh was an aromatic gum from which perfume was drawn. It was used in preparing corpses for burial (among other things). Again, Jesus as a child had no use for this. It was given in anticipation of the purpose for His coming and that was to die as an atonement for sin.

The gifts were given to reflect who the child really was in a witness of faith (He was king, He was God, He was sacrifice).

After this time with Jesus, Matthew informs us that the wise men are warned by God in a dream to avoid Herod, and so they make their way home by a different route.

Herod – The Earthly King

Throughout this narrative we see the hand of Herod trying to manipulate the wise men in order to gain information for his own murderous ends. Herod was not beyond killing his own family members in order to secure his throne. He had received his position from the Romans, and in receiving the title "King of the Jews" had violated God's word in displacing David's heirs from ruling God's people. He was not fully Jewish and was not of David's royal lineage, yet he ruled in the name of a pagan emperor. Herod understood this enough to know that there had been a Messiah promised by God and that He was sent to rule the people.

And so this evil king took the wise men's search seriously, to the point that he was going to try to find and destroy the child they sought. We read in the rest of the chapter that in an effort to do so, he has every male child two years and under killed in Bethlehem just in case. What is so strange about his behavior is that if the prophecy concerning the Messiah was being fulfilled by the birth of this child, how did he ever think he could stop God's hand?

Summary

Matthew opens his gospel with a very brief description of Jesus' physical birth and earthly background. He also demonstrates that from the very beginning Jesus was recognized and honored by the Magi as:

1. **The Messiah** – They searched for Him according to the prophecies concerning the divine Messiah and Savior.

2. **The King** – They recognized that as the Messiah He also carried the title of King.

3. **The Sacrifice** – Their gift of myrrh pointed to the ultimate task of the Messiah, which was to die for His people.

This episode sets the tone for the rest of Matthew's gospel where he continues to describe Jesus with the imagery of king and ruler. Although this is not a parable or a teaching section, there are certain practical lessons we can draw from this encounter between the wise men and the royal child.

God uses many ways to reach people

He used a method that these men could relate to (a star in the heavens) in order to lead them to Christ. Sometimes He uses a tract left on a bus, an ad in a newspaper, an invitation by a friend, an illness, a service, a TV show, a website, a missionary, a letter, or whatever. God has a million ways to reach out to someone who needs Christ.

Our job is not to decide ahead of time what will work and what won't; our job is to keep trying until it works or until Jesus comes.

Salvation is by faith

Even though they saw an amazing star, they had to pack their bags and head out – that required faith. Even though the Jewish teachers said that the Messiah was supposed to be in Bethlehem and not Jerusalem (which made more sense to them) they had to leave sense behind and try to find Him in Bethlehem – that required faith. Even though everything pointed to this baby Jesus as the King, the poor house and the poor parents didn't lend much credibility to this fact. For them to bow down and worship the child of these poorest of people required faith.

Today we can't see a star and we can't touch the babe, but God calls us through His word to come to Jesus in repentance and baptism – that step forward always requires faith.

The word is the only guide to Jesus

Although the special star played a role in finding the babe – the word is what truly led them to Him. Daniel's words long before had captured their hearts and set them looking for God's Messiah. Micah's words confirmed the birthplace of the true Messiah. God's word through the angel kept them and the baby safe from Herod.

We need to be careful not to let feelings, coincidences, opinions or signs lead our spiritual lives. We live by every word that comes from the mouth of God – not signs, traditions or feelings. We must test everything against God's word; it is the standard for truth, for what is right and pleasing to God.

We believe Jesus is King because the word of God tells us this. This belief then is sure and will never be changed.

CHAPTER 2
THE KING'S TEMPTATION

MATTHEW 4:1-11

We are studying the book of Matthew and his perspective of Jesus as Divine King. We began by reviewing the first instance in Matthew where the gospel writer portrays Jesus as a royal or kingly figure, and that was at His birth where He was worshiped by the wise men from Babylon and presented with gifts that represented His royal, divine and sacrificial character. Matthew continues his description of Jesus' life with an unusual episode where Jesus is tempted by the devil. This event occurred immediately after He was baptized by John and confirmed as the Divine Messiah by the appearance of the Holy Spirit and the voice of God.

This begins Jesus's public ministry on a lofty note, but to balance out the view, we now see Jesus in the desert being hungry, thirsty, tired and battling temptation. In this scene,

Matthew is able to show us that even though Jesus is King, He must face the same attacks from the same opponent as we do. Of course, as Divine King, He is able to demonstrate His mastery over Satan and all of His temptations.

This same story is told in Mark and Luke's gospel, but Matthew's description is the most complete.

> Then Jesus was led up by the Spirit into the wilderness to be tempted by the devil.
> - Matthew 4:1

Mark says that Jesus was "impelled " by the spirit. Later on in His ministry Jesus said that He only spoke and did what the Father told Him to speak and do (John 8:28-29). This guidance, as we see here, was provided through the agency of the Holy Spirit. This was no human desire (to go into the desert to face the treacherous temptation of Satan). Human nature would have avoided a deadly confrontation with such an opponent so early in one's ministry. Human nature would have capitalized on the great events at His baptism in order to start a successful ministry. Human nature would have developed a strong following as well as greater strength and wisdom in ministry before going one-on-one with Satan. But Jesus' ministry was totally devoted to God, and it was God's will that this test be faced at once. Without delay then, Jesus goes into the desert immediately following His baptism.

> And after He had fasted forty days and forty nights, He then became hungry.
> - Matthew 4:2

Mark says that during these forty days in the desert Jesus was tempted by Satan and was with wild beasts. The way Matthew and Mark describe it, Jesus' experience in the desert was as follows:

1. He fasted

No food for 40 days. Since He had no weaknesses of the body and soul caused by sin, He only became hungry after 40 days.

2. He was with wild beats

Mark is the one who mentions this and it could be a reference to animals or the continuous temptations He had to endure. The way the passage is written in Matthew suggests that He faced 40 days of continuous harassment from Satan and his allies.

3. He defeats Satan

By the end of the 40 days of fasting He becomes hungry, and at this point Satan himself attempts to destroy Him. There may have been other instances and encounters with the Devil, but this is the one preserved and revealed to us.

4. He is ministered to by angels

I'll speak more about this later, but for now suffice to say that the Father provides for Jesus' needs through angels. Before we go on to Satan's three temptations, let's discuss the nature of these temptations with regard to Jesus. In the book of James, James describes the nature of temptation on an ordinary person:

> But each one is tempted when he is carried away and enticed by his own lust. Then when lust has conceived, it gives birth to sin; and when sin is accomplished, it brings forth death.
> - James 1:14-15

In this passage James refers to the type of temptation that calls on a corresponding weakness in a person in order to seduce them into sin. That is to say:

- Alcohol for the alcoholic
- Opportunity to boast in the one who is conceited
- Pornography for the urge to lust

So in one form, temptation is a seduction, a luring into the trap of sin and resulting death by using or offering something or someone that corresponds to a forbidden desire within the individual. This was not the nature of Satan's temptations on Jesus because the Bible also teaches that God cannot be tempted by evil (James 1:13) and Jesus is God.

The temptations that Jesus struggled with, therefore, were tests, were things done to examine and produce His true self. They were ways to reveal weaknesses, inconsistencies and hypocrisies. For example:

- Humans experience these "tests" or temptations whenever they fill out a form, write an exam or suffer some kind of adversity.
- These things are tests/temptations that bring out our true character.

Satan's temptations were not allurements to Jesus's sinful nature, He was without sin and so nothing would seduce him. Satan's temptations were tests to measure the claims and person of Christ to see if he could discredit, discourage, or distract Him from His Father's command to carry out His ministry on our behalf. Satan had ruined the first Adam and now would use his full force to try and stop Adam's savior, Jesus.

Temptation #1 – Prove Yourself

> And the tempter came and said to Him, "If You are the Son of God, command that these stones become bread." But He answered and said, "It is written, 'Man shall not live on bread alone, but on every word that proceeds out of the mouth of God.'"
> - Matthew 4:3-4

On the surface this seems like a reasonable request: if you are the Son of God, then give me the kind of proof that only such a person could provide. The "test" here was to see if Jesus would rely on God's word for proof of this or exercise some form of power to confirm this fact. Before entering the desert the Father said from heaven:

> This is my beloved Son in whom I am will pleased
> - Matthew 3:17

Was God's "word" enough, or did Jesus need to supply more – for Himself or for others? If Jesus provided the miracle (which He was perfectly capable of doing), He would be doing the same thing the Jews did afterwards: relying on signs and wonders to prove God's word, rather than simply relying on the credibility of His word alone. Jesus' answer (from Deuteronomy 8:3) is at once concise and all encompassing:

- It is taken from Moses' summary of exhortation to the Israelites before they entered the Promised Land.

- They had been miraculously freed from Egyptian slavery and miraculously sustained in the desert for 40 years with the bread of manna from heaven.

- An entire generation witnessed great miracles from God, and yet Moses warns them that their lives were sustained by God's word, not by His miracles.
- In other words, the miracles served the word and not the other way around. For example:
    - God had promised in His word to Abraham and others that He would eventually give them the Promised Land. The miracles simply brought His word to its fulfillment.
    - God told the Israelites that He would save and bless them and that His word was the guarantee that it would happen – not the miracles.

God's word declared that Jesus was the Son of God and that word was the absolute and final proof anyone needed for this to be established. The test was to see if Jesus would go beyond the word of the Father. Jesus quotes the very words of the Father that establish the all sufficiency of God's word. In other words, Jesus tells Satan that God's word says that I am the Son of God, and that is enough proof.

Temptation #2 – Prove the Word

> Then the Devil took Him into the holy city and had Him stand on the pinnacle of the temple, and said to Him, "If You are the Son of God, throw Yourself down; for it is written, 'He will command his angels concerning you'; and 'On their hands they will bear you up, so that you will not strike your foot against a stone.'"
> Jesus said to him, "On the other hand, it is written, 'You shall not put the Lord your God to the test.'"
> - Matthew 4:5-7

Satan is unbowed and unrepentant at Jesus' response to his first attack. He merely follows it up with a subsequent ploy, this time based on the word of God itself. At first he says, "prove yourself" and Jesus replies, "the word proves Me and who I am." So Satan comes back with "prove the word" in a way that would put Jesus' human form in danger.

Josephus, a Jewish historian of the time, writes that there was a point on the exterior wall surrounding the temple (Solomon's Porch) where the drop to the ravine below was 600 feet. Satan's suggestion was that if the word is your proof, test it to see if what it says about you is true. The passage is from Psalms 91:11-12 and refers to God's providential care of not only His Divine Son but also all of His children of faith.

- The deception is not in misquoting the passage. The deception lies in using this passage to prove a false promise.

- The passage teaches that God uses extraordinary means (even angels) to care for and protect His children.

- Satan, however, uses this passage to suggest the idea that God will protect and preserve you no matter what you do.

In response, Jesus correctly discerns Satan's intent and answers with a scripture that addresses the true issue: presumptuousness. His scripture reference does not contradict the passage set forth by Satan, it explains it fully so that the meaning is clear. Yes, we are to trust God's promise to care for us, but to foolishly test God's promise with careless actions is presumptuous and full of pride. This type of action is an attempt to force God to prove His promise, and in doing this one shows a lack of trust as well as a proud heart.

The first test was to see if Jesus would provide a sign to prove Himself, and the second test was to see if Jesus would ask the Father to provide a sign to prove His word. In both responses Jesus relies on the word and its proper meaning to meet Satan's attacks.

Temptation #3 - Take The Easy Way

> Again, the devil took Him to a very high mountain and showed Him all the kingdoms of the world and their glory, and he said to Him, "All these things I will give You, if You fall down and worship me."
> Then Jesus said to him, "Go, Satan! For it is written, 'you shall worship the Lord your God, and serve Him only.'"
> - Matthew 4:8-10

In the first two tests, the issue rested upon Jesus' divine nature and His relationship to the Father and His word. This third attempt appeals more to Jesus' human nature and His mission here as the Messiah and King. This is where our theme of Jesus as King shines through in this passage. Matthew has already established Jesus' credentials as Divine King with his description of the wise men's gifts and worship.

Here Satan offers Jesus a position that the Lord already has: King over all kingdoms. Of course, Satan's deceit is evident in several ways:

- He falsely claims that all of the kingdoms have been given to him. He rules in this world as a rebel leader in disobedience to God, they haven't been given.

- He also falsely claims that he has the power to crown Jesus Lord over these, but he has no such power or authority from God.

In suggesting that he will do this if Jesus worships him, Satan is offering Jesus a crown without having to suffer a cross.

Jesus is crowned Lord of all because of His victory over sin and death through His cross and resurrection.

> who will transform the body of our humble state into conformity with the body of His glory, by the exertion of the power that He has even to subject all things to Himself.
> - Philippians 3:21

Satan falsely appeals to Him to forgo this route for the easier way of simply changing His allegiance.

- Why suffer to become king?
- Worship me and you receive the same thing without suffering.

It was the same lie that made Adam and Eve fall (you shall become like gods if you do as I say). Of course, they wouldn't have, and didn't, they simply lost what they already had! Jesus was king, a king with a mission from the Father. He answered the way Eve and Adam should have responded: "Be gone, Satan!"

Jesus, for the first time, addresses the Devil and rebukes him openly. His command is such for two reasons:

- He had exhausted his temptations and lost, and it was time for him to go.
- He had offered the worst temptation of all: to deny God, to break the first commandment by denying the Father. In Jesus' case this would be to try and achieve His mission by denying the Father's plan of salvation.

The test was to see if Jesus would carry out the Father's plan (death on the cross to gain forgiveness for man) or Satan's plan (worship Satan and gain rulership). In His reply, Jesus not only vanquishes the Devil and his schemes, but also guarantees the salvation of all those whose hope rested on Him and His sacrifice.

> Then the devil left Him; and behold, angels came and began to minister to Him.
> - Matthew 4:11

Matthew describes angels ministering to the Lord, the King:

- Their assistance would have been to provide food and sustenance.

- To return Him to His home.

- To celebrate and rejoice with Him this great and desired spiritual battle (who else could understand at this point?).

Satan continued to attack Jesus through others eventually causing His death, but his own power was tested and defeated once and for all at this critical point in Jesus' ministry.

Lessons

1. Jesus is king of the spiritual world

In the description of the wise men's appearance, Matthew establishes Jesus as a royal figure recognized by worldly leaders, and whether they were friendly, like the Magi, or enemies, like Herod, they both recognized His royal position.

Here he shows that Jesus is also king or ruler over the spiritual world as well. He defeats Satan, the supreme spiritual enemy. He is served by angels, the supreme spiritual ministers. Either way, Jesus is the ruler.

2. The word of God saves

It is through the word that we come to save our souls (Romans 1:16). It is also through the word that we remain saved (Matthew 4:1-11, II Timothy 3:16).

Knowing the word, knowing it in context, using it and applying it properly will keep our spiritual lives healthy and safe from the many temptations of the evil one. The purpose of our teaching, preaching and regular Bible reading as well as our prayers is to keep souls strong and safe through the knowledge of God's word.

CHAPTER 3
THE KINGDOM CHARACTER

MATTHEW 5:1-16

So far in our study of Jesus in Matthew we have focused on Jesus as the king; the perspective in which Matthew presents Him in his gospel. We see Him as the king worshiped by human rulers at His birth as the wise men were led to do so by the star sent to them by God.

We witnessed His rulership over the dark spiritual forces led by Satan as He defeats the devil in his effort to tempt Him in the desert. Our last glimpse is of the sovereign ruler, Jesus, being ministered to by mighty angelic beings—showing us His rulership over the entire spiritual world, both good and bad.

In the following section of his book, Matthew will now turn his attention to the kingdom over which Jesus rules. This kingdom will be explained and described under the heading, "Sermon on the Mount," because of the time and location that Jesus, the king, begins speaking about His kingdom.

The Kingdom of the King

The Sermon on the Mount begins in chapter five of Matthew and ends in chapter seven. In this sermon or lesson Jesus explains the attitude, the character, the impact, and the relationships that those people, who make up His kingdom, have. Jesus' kingdom, we will see, is not a geopolitical entity, it's not a place or a culture. His kingdom can be made up of one person or a million people together because it exists within the heart, not on a map.

Jesus' kingdom exists wherever His will is being done. So if His will is being done in your heart, His kingdom is within you. If His will is being done within the heart of a thousand or a billion people, His kingdom exists among them. This explains what the kingdom of Jesus is but not what it looks like or how it acts.

We see then that in the Sermon on the Mount, the king answers the question, "How do people act when they have the kingdom within them?" or, "When this kingdom is established in one or a thousand hearts, what difference does it make; how do we recognize it?" Jesus answers these questions about His kingdom by comparing and describing the life in the kingdom to life in the world, in five different areas. These areas, that everyone could relate to, were the following:

1. True happiness
2. Attitude towards the Law
3. Relationship with God
4. Relationship with others
5. Life in the kingdom

With these teachings Jesus was describing the nature and experience one could expect in the kingdom over which he was king.

What Constitutes Real Happiness (Beatitudes)

When Jesus saw the crowds, He went up on the mountain; and after He sat down, His disciples came to Him. He opened His mouth and began to teach them, saying,

"Blessed are the poor in spirit, for theirs is the kingdom of heaven.

"Blessed are those who mourn, for they shall be comforted.

"Blessed are the gentle, for they shall inherit the earth.

"Blessed are those who hunger and thirst for righteousness, for they shall be satisfied.

"Blessed are the merciful, for they shall receive mercy.

"Blessed are the pure in heart, for they shall see God.

"Blessed are the peacemakers, for they shall be called sons of God.

"Blessed are those who have been persecuted for the sake of righteousness, for theirs is the kingdom of heaven.

"Blessed are you when people insult you and persecute you, and falsely say all kinds of evil against you because of Me. Rejoice and be glad, for your reward in heaven is great; for in the same way they persecuted the prophets who were before you.

"You are the salt of the earth; but if the salt has become

tasteless, how can it be made salty again? It is no longer good for anything, except to be thrown out and trampled under foot by men.

"You are the light of the world. A city set on a hill cannot be hidden; nor does anyone light a lamp and put it under a basket, but on the lampstand, and it gives light to all who are in the house. Let your light shine before men in such a way that they may see your good works, and glorify your Father who is in heaven.
- Matthew 5:1-16

The word beatitude does not appear in the New Testament as such; it is a Latin translation (beatitudo) for the word blessed, meaning happy or joyful.

There are nine beatitudes and all begin the same way: they make a promise, deal with spiritual things and are directed at people in the kingdom since they make no sense to non-Christians. They were spoken in a style of teaching that Rabbis usually had in introducing their lesson with a question or a paradox. Beatitudes were contradictions which challenged the preconceived notions of life and philosophy. That is to say:

- Spiritually poor attain riches of heaven
- Mourners will be comforted
- Gentle will gain earth (not warriors)
- Thirsty will be satisfied, etc.

In the beatitudes Jesus gives insight into the spiritual reality that operates in the kingdom of heaven. They are spiritual principles by which we, in the kingdom, operate.

For example, in the kingdom those who bear persecution in the name of Christ do rejoice. This is not the normal reaction for those who are persecuted. People in this situation are usually afraid, angry or have a desire for revenge. However, in the kingdom, the spiritual laws work in such a way that those who suffer for Christ rejoice in Him. Disciples who are influenced by these principles become distinctive (like salt as a flavor, and light to the eye are distinctive).

True happiness (blessedness) therefore is distinctive. The distinctiveness of the disciples, characterized by the principles set forth in the beatitudes, is what makes them stand apart from others and what characterizes the kingdom (like the saltiness of salt or the brightness of light). The happiness of those in the kingdom is based on God's will being accomplished through and in them regardless of the consequences. This distinctiveness, ultimately perceived in good lives and good works, not only characterizes the kingdom, but reveals the true nature of God to fellow man.

What makes you happy in the kingdom is very different than what makes you happy in the world.

In the beatitudes we see man as he is in the regenerated state, and that state is blessed.

How do Kingdom Dwellers Relate to the Law – Matthew 5:17-48

> "Do not think that I came to abolish the Law or the Prophets; I did not come to abolish but to fulfill. For truly I say to you, until heaven and earth pass away, not the smallest letter or stroke shall pass from the Law until all is accomplished. Whoever then annuls one of the least of these commandments, and teaches others to do the same, shall be called least in the kingdom of heaven; but whoever keeps and teaches them, he shall be called great in the kingdom of heaven.

> For I say to you that unless your righteousness surpasses that of the scribes and Pharisees, you will not enter the kingdom of heaven."
> - Matthew 5:17-20

The key verse in the discourse is verse 20. It reveals that the higher righteousness of the disciples is the quality that distinguishes them and makes them useful in the kingdom setting them apart from those who dwell in the world. From verses 17-48 He makes a series of comparisons putting forth what they had been taught about the Law of Moses by their teachers, "...you have heard that it was said..." and lays beside these teachings the *essence* and *spirit* of the Law given by the one who originally gave the Law to Moses: Jesus Himself. The Lord comments on five areas of teaching in which they had received instructions concerning the Law:

1. Murder
The unjustified taking of life was wrong.

> "You have heard that the ancients were told, 'You shall not commit murder,' and 'Whoever commits murder shall be liable to the court.' But I say to you that everyone who is angry with his brother shall be guilty before the court; and whoever says to his brother, 'You good-for-nothing,' shall be guilty before the supreme court; and whoever says, 'You fool,' shall be guilty enough to go into the fiery hell."
> - Matthew 5:21-22

Jesus establishes the breaking of the command at the beginning of anger and resentment towards others and that keeping the Law meant that one made a conscious effort at reconciliation, not just avoiding murder—the extreme. The teachers taught that if you avoided the extreme, you obeyed the whole Law.

2. Adultery
They had been taught to manipulate the Law in order to justify their adultery with easy divorce.

> "You have heard that it was said, 'You shall not commit adultery,' but I say to you that everyone who looks at a woman with lust for her has already committed adultery with her in his heart.
> - Matthew 5:27-28

Jesus again situates the true sin as impurity of heart and the actual keeping of the Law as an effort to control one's body, not manipulation of the Law in order to gain easy divorces.

3. Vows
They had learned a complex manner of making selective vows which they felt they could break when inconvenient.

> "Again, you have heard that the ancients were told, 'YOU SHALL NOT MAKE FALSE VOWS, BUT SHALL FULFILL YOUR VOWS TO THE LORD.'
> ...
> "But let your statement be, 'Yes, yes' or 'No, no'; anything beyond these is of evil."
> - Matthew 5:33,37

Jesus reveals that vows are not necessary when one has an honest heart; real obedience required love and honesty.

4. Justice
Their system relied on the Law as a tool for restitution and many times a cover for revenge.

> "You have heard that it was said, 'An eye for an eye, and a tooth for a tooth.'"
> - Matthew 5:38

Jesus taught them that the higher principle of the Law was mercy not justice.

5. Humanity
They used the Law to build a wall around themselves and keep others out.

> "You have heard that it was said, 'You shall love your neighbor and hate your enemy.' "But I say to you, love your enemies and pray for those who persecute you…"
> - Matthew 5:43-44

Jesus showed them that one purpose of the Law was to reveal God's goodness to men, that to be like the giver of the Law, they had to love enemies as He had done with them.

And so, in the kingdom there exists both a true understanding of the essence of God's Law and a sincere desire to abide by the spirit of the Law. In the kingdom there is no game playing: God's word, His will and His Law is life itself, and there is a true hunger to do what is right. Some have made a rule book out of this passage thinking that in order to be in the kingdom you had to perfectly obey the standard that Jesus speaks about here. This idea and practice somehow replaces the old Law with a new and harder one to obey.

What these well meaning but misguided individuals misunderstand is that through the grace of God obtained by Jesus on the cross we are considered perfect according to the kingdom standards outlined here by faith, not by perfect obedience (which is impossible for sinful man). In other words, when God looks at the members of the kingdom, this is the perfection He sees – not because the people in the kingdom have achieved it, but because the king of the kingdom has achieved it for His subjects by dying on the cross. When Jesus teaches blessed are those who hunger and thirst for rightness, for they shall be satisfied – this is what He's talking about.

- The righteousness is the perfection He describes in these passages concerning the Law.

- If this is what you hunger for, you will be given it through faith in Him and thus be satisfied.

- This is the cause of your blessedness, your happiness.

- That you hunger for something you could not achieve for yourself – and Jesus gives it to you because you believe in Him.

The kingdom dwellers understand and perfectly obey the Law through faith in Jesus Christ.

> But by His doing you are in Christ Jesus, who became to us wisdom from God, and righteousness and sanctification, and redemption.
> - I Corinthians 1:30

In the kingdom what really brings happiness is obeying the true essence of the Law, and through faith in Christ this is made possible!

Relationship with God

> "Beware of practicing your righteousness before men to be noticed by them; otherwise you have no reward with your Father who is in heaven.
>
> "So when you give to the poor, do not sound a trumpet before you, as the hypocrites do in the synagogues and in the streets, so that they may be honored by men. Truly I say to you, they have their reward in full.
>
> "But when you give to the poor, do not let your left hand know what your right hand is doing, so that your giving will be in secret; and your Father who sees what is done in secret will reward you."
> - Matthew 6:1-4

Jesus goes on to teach them how those in the kingdom exercise their relationship with God.

In the world, religion consists mainly of ritual, repetition and tradition. In the kingdom however we do the following:

1. We practice goodness towards God with a view of pleasing Him, not men. (vs. 1-4)

2. We pray to God in order to communicate with Him, not to impress others with our piety. (vs. 5-18)

3. Trust God to provide all of our physical and spiritual needs, not ourselves or the world. (vs. 19-34)

Jesus teaches them to understand the nature of the kingdom (beatitudes), the quality of life that they should strive for as salt and light of the earth (essence of the Law), and now guides them into the practical ways of how to have a meaningful relationship with Himself as opposed to the various methods offered by the world to achieve this end.

Relationship with Others

> "Do not judge so that you will not be judged. For in the way you judge, you will be judged; and by your standard of measure, it will be measured to you. Why do you look at the speck that is in your brother's eye, but do not notice the log that is in your own eye? Or how can you say to your brother, 'Let me take the speck out of your eye,' and behold, the log is in your own eye? You hypocrite, first take the log out of your own eye, and then you will see clearly to take the speck out of your brother's eye.
>
> "Do not give what is holy to dogs, and do not throw your pearls before swine, or they will trample them under their feet, and turn and tear you to pieces.
>
> "Ask, and it will be given to you; seek, and you will find; knock, and it will be opened to you. For everyone who asks receives, and he who seeks finds, and to him who knocks it will be opened. Or what man is there among you who, when his son asks for a loaf, will give him a stone? Or if he asks for a fish, he will not give him a snake, will he? If you then, being evil, know how to give good gifts to your children, how much more will your Father who is in heaven give what is good to those who ask Him!
>
> "In everything, therefore, treat people the same way you want them to treat you, for this is the Law and the Prophets."
> - Matthew 7:1-12

The elements for a proper relationship with God are followed by the key idea to a blessed relationship between people in the kingdom.

> "In everything, therefore, treat people the same way you want them to treat you, for this is the Law and the Prophets."
> - Matthew 7:12

All the teaching contained in the Law and the Prophets can be summarized by this one principle. In it one learns how to treat others in ways that bless our relationships with God and man. This "golden rule" as some refer to it also instructs those in the kingdom on the very practical way to keep the kingdom alive within themselves and please God as a result. Note also how differently those in the world treat one another and the sad results seen in every age.

The Way of Life

> "Enter through the narrow gate; for the gate is wide and the way is broad that leads to destruction, and there are many who enter through it. For the gate is small and the way is narrow that leads to life, and there are few who find it.
>
> "Beware of the false prophets, who come to you in sheep's clothing, but inwardly are ravenous wolves.
>
> "You will know them by their fruits. Grapes are not gathered from thorn bushes nor figs from thistles, are they? So every good tree bears good fruit, but the bad tree bears bad fruit. A good tree cannot produce bad fruit, nor can a bad tree produce good fruit. Every tree that does not bear good fruit is cut down and thrown into the fire. So then, you will know them by their fruits.

> "Not everyone who says to Me, 'Lord, Lord,' will enter the kingdom of heaven, but he who does the will of My Father who is in heaven will enter. Many will say to Me on that day, 'Lord, Lord, did we not prophesy in Your name, and in Your name cast out demons, and in Your name perform many miracles?' And then I will declare to them, 'I never knew you; depart from me, you who practice lawlessness.'
>
> "Therefore everyone who hears these words of Mine and acts on them, may be compared to a wise man who built his house on the rock. And the rain fell, and the floods came, and the winds blew and slammed against that house; and yet it did not fall, for it had been founded on the rock. Everyone who hears these words of Mine and does not act on them, will be like a foolish man who built his house on the sand. The rain fell, and the floods came, and the winds blew and slammed against that house; and it fell—and great was its fall." When Jesus had finished these words, the crowds were amazed at His teaching; for He was teaching them as one having authority, and not as their scribes.
> - Matthew 7:13-29

Having set forth the parameters of the kingdom and its inner workings, Jesus explains the way to enter into the kingdom and into a relationship with the king and the Father as a result. (vs. 13-15) This is His invitation to His audience:

1. Enter by the narrow gate of Christ.

Later on at His crucifixion the disciples will understand just how narrow and difficult this gate is. The only way to God and the kingdom of Christ is through a response to the cross.

2. Beware of false prophets who produce neither the teachings nor the fruit of the kingdom of Christ.

That's how you know them, neither the fruit nor the teaching. True prophets have the fruit and the teachings. Don't be fooled by those who produce some of the fruit but don't have the teaching, and vice versa. Prophets need both!

3. Don't just hear the words of Christ, act upon them in order to enter in.

Many are called but few become the chosen ones who belong to the kingdom. Many heard all of what He said that day and were amazed, but few entered through the narrow gate of the cross into the kingdom of the king.

Thus ends Jesus' comprehensive description of His heavenly kingdom as it would appear in a physical context among men.

CHAPTER 4
THE KING IN ACTION

MATTHEW 8:1-9:38

In the previous chapter we focused on the idea of the "kingdom." We looked at the kingdom over which the King presided. This kingdom was not physical or political in nature. I said that it existed wherever the will of Jesus was being done, and wherever Jesus' will was being done the following things existed because of it:

- True happiness or blessedness
- True righteousness before God
- True relationship between God and man
- True response to His word

In the following section, Matthew returns his attention to the King Himself and describes the incredible pace and impact of the King as He carries out His ministry in establishing His kingdom.

In John 21:25 the Apostle says that the world could not contain all the books if all of what Jesus did was recorded. This is certainly true when you examine the millions of books written about Jesus and His life and written only about the small amount of material given to us about Him in the Bible. In chapters 8 and 9 of Matthew's gospel, Matthew describes three very hectic days in the life of Jesus; three days filled with travel, miracles and teachings. All of which are given as a glimpse into Jesus' spectacular ministry, as the King works at establishing His kingdom among men. Matthew does not lay out these events in chronological order, he groups them into blocks of miracles and teaching:

1. Three miracles
2. Teaching
3. Three miracles
4. Teaching
5. Four miracles
6. Summary teaching

This arrangement doesn't describe the flow of events as they happened each day but they are easier to remember for teaching purposes. In these two action-packed chapters, Mathew describes ten miracles and three sets of teachings by the Lord.

The teachings have a variety of topics, but the most important one is that of discipleship. Matthew has described:

- The birth of the king
- The witness of His rule from men, angels and God Himself
- The nature of His kingdom
- The way into His kingdom

Now He describes the way Jesus went about calling men into the kingdom and into the service of the kingdom.

Narrative

We begin in chapter 8 as Matthew describes the first group of miracles followed by a teaching.

Miracles

1. Leper cleansed

> When Jesus came down from the mountain, large crowds followed Him. ² And a leper came to Him and bowed down before Him, and said, "Lord, if You are willing, You can make me clean." ³ Jesus stretched out His hand and touched him, saying, "I am willing; be cleansed." And immediately his leprosy was cleansed. ⁴ And Jesus said to him, "See that you tell no one; but go, show yourself to the priest and present the offering that Moses commanded, as a testimony to them."
> - Matthew 8:1-4

The leper demonstrated his faith: He believed that Jesus could heal him and experienced instant healing as a result. Jesus "touched" him and he went from being unclean to clean. The leper had to show himself to a priest in order to confirm his cleansing. This confirmation would then permit him to re-enter the social and worship life that he had been denied because of his affliction.

2. Centurion's slave

> [5] And when Jesus entered Capernaum, a centurion came to Him, imploring Him, [6] and saying, "Lord, my servant is lying paralyzed at home, fearfully tormented." [7] Jesus said to him, "I will come and heal him." [8] But the centurion said, "Lord, I am not worthy for You to come under my roof, but just say the word, and my servant will be healed. [9] For I also am a man under authority, with soldiers under me; and I say to this one, 'Go!' and he goes, and to another, 'Come!' and he comes, and to my slave, 'Do this!' and he does it." [10] Now when Jesus heard this, He marveled and said to those who were following, "Truly I say to you, I have not found such great faith with anyone in Israel. [11] I say to you that many will come from east and west, and recline at the table with Abraham, Isaac and Jacob in the kingdom of heaven; [12] but the sons of the kingdom will be cast out into the outer darkness; in that place there will be weeping and gnashing of teeth." [13] And Jesus said to the centurion, "Go; it shall be done for you as you have believed." And the servant was healed that very moment.
> - Matthew 8:5-13

The centurion was a pious proselyte (convert to Judaism). He addressed Jesus as Lord demonstrating his faith. He took Jesus at His word. Jesus marvels at the quality of His faith (imagine impressing Jesus!). His servant is healed by Jesus' word, not personal willingness or faith.

3. Healings

> [14] When Jesus came into Peter's home, He saw his mother-in-law lying sick in bed with a fever. [15] He touched her hand, and the fever left her; and she got up

and waited on Him. [16] When evening came, they brought to Him many who were demon-possessed; and He cast out the spirits with a word, and healed all who were ill. [17] This was to fulfill what was spoken through Isaiah the prophet: "He Himself took our infirmities and carried away our diseases."
- Matthew 8:14-17

She was healed immediately and completely without discourse. Many are brought to Jesus with physical, emotional or spiritual ailments and are healed. Matthew shows that this miraculous healing power of Jesus was in accord with prophecy concerning the Messiah.

Teaching

[18] Now when Jesus saw a crowd around Him, He gave orders to depart to the other side of the sea. [19] Then a scribe came and said to Him, "Teacher, I will follow You wherever You go." [20] Jesus said to him, "The foxes have holes and the birds of the air have nests, but the Son of Man has nowhere to lay His head." [21] Another of the disciples said to Him, "Lord, permit me first to go and bury my father." [22] But Jesus said to him, "Follow Me, and allow the dead to bury their own dead."
- Matthew 8:18-22

Instruction to would-be disciples

He warns them of the "other worldly" experience of the kingdom. Those in the kingdom are in the world but have difficulty being a part of it. They never really feel "at home." They are only pilgrims passing through.

This was especially true for a Jewish scribe whose identity was tied up with history, culture and geography. It would be hard to identify with Christ rather than a physical religion bound in history. Disciples make their home here, but they are not at home until they are with Christ.

Dead bury the dead – what does this mean? Let the spiritually dead worry about the things of the world; don't let these things hold you back from following Christ.

Miracles

Matthew goes on to describe another group of miracles:

4. Calming the storm

> [23] When He got into the boat, His disciples followed Him. [24] And behold, there arose a great storm on the sea, so that the boat was being covered with the waves; but Jesus Himself was asleep. [25] And they came to Him and woke Him, saying, "Save us, Lord; we are perishing!" [26] He said to them, "Why are you afraid, you men of little faith?" Then He got up and rebuked the winds and the sea, and it became perfectly calm. [27] The men were amazed, and said, "What kind of a man is this, that even the winds and the sea obey Him?"
> - Matthew 8:23-27

They appealed to Jesus to save them from the storm. They had little faith, not no faith, and weakness demonstrated in fear. Jesus' power over nature has never been duplicated by any ancient or modern faith healer. No self-proclaimed miracle worker has ever demonstrated this type of power.

5. Cast out demons

> [28] When He came to the other side into the country of the Gadarenes, two men who were demon-possessed met Him as they were coming out of the tombs. They were so extremely violent that no one could pass by that way. [29] And they cried out, saying, "What business do we have with each other, Son of God? Have You come here to torment us before the time?" [30] Now there was a herd of many swine feeding at a distance from them. [31] The demons began to entreat Him, saying, "If You are going to cast us out, send us into the herd of swine." [32] And He said to them, "Go!" And they came out and went into the swine, and the whole herd rushed down the steep bank into the sea and perished in the waters. [33] The herdsmen ran away, and went to the city and reported everything, including what had happened to the demoniacs. [34] And behold, the whole city came out to meet Jesus; and when they saw Him, they implored Him to leave their region.
> - Matthew 8:28-34

These demons were dangerous and the man was possessed by many of these. The demons feared that their judgment was at hand (they knew the results but not the time). No one knows the time. If the spirits don't know, then certainly man doesn't either. Jesus casts these spirits out with simply a word. The evil spirits cause the swine to run into the lake and drown.

6. Paralytic cured

> [1] Getting into a boat, Jesus crossed over the sea and came to His own city. [2] And they brought to Him a paralytic lying on a bed. Seeing their faith, Jesus said to the paralytic, "Take courage, son; your sins are

> forgiven." ³ And some of the scribes said to themselves, "This fellow blasphemes." ⁴ And Jesus knowing their thoughts said, "Why are you thinking evil in your hearts? ⁵ Which is easier, to say, 'Your sins are forgiven,' or to say, 'Get up, and walk'? ⁶ But so that you may know that the Son of Man has authority on earth to forgive sins"—then He said to the paralytic, "Get up, pick up your bed and go home." ⁷ And he got up and went home. ⁸ But when the crowds saw this, they were awestruck, and glorified God, who had given such authority to men.
> - Matthew 9:1-8

First Jesus forgives his sins. The scribes grumble because they feel Jesus has no right or power to do this (only God). They accuse Him of blasphemy. Jesus demonstrates His right and power by healing the man's disease (power over one demonstrates and confirms power over the other). The people glorify God. That people give glory to God is one of the main purposes for miracles. These signs were never meant to make the miracle workers rich!

Teaching

Matthew is called

> As Jesus went on from there, He saw a man called Matthew, sitting in the tax collector's booth; and He said to him, "Follow Me!" And he got up and followed Him.
> - Matthew 9:9

Note how simply he writes about his own call and response. Matthew gives his name, his former life (tax collector), his call and response. He uses the third person to tell his own story and provides no dialogue from Jesus to himself. This demonstrates his genuine humility.

Accusation of eating with sinners

> [10] Then it happened that as Jesus was reclining at the table in the house, behold, many tax collectors and sinners came and were dining with Jesus and His disciples. [11] When the Pharisees saw this, they said to His disciples, "Why is your Teacher eating with the tax collectors and sinners?" [12] But when Jesus heard this, He said, "It is not those who are healthy who need a physician, but those who are sick. [13] But go and learn what this means: 'I desire compassion, and not sacrifice,' for I did not come to call the righteous, but sinners."
> - Matthew 9:10-13

Jesus' response was that His ministry was one of comparison not ceremony. The miracles of healing and the ministry of the cross were motivated by compassion in order to glorify God in the saving of souls. Nothing glorifies God more than soul saving and service.

John's disciples

> [14] Then the disciples of John came to Him, asking, "Why do we and the Pharisees fast, but Your disciples do not fast?" [15] And Jesus said to them, "The attendants of the bridegroom cannot mourn as long as the bridegroom is with them, can they? But the days will come when the bridegroom is taken away from them, and then they will fast. [16] But no one puts a patch of unshrunk cloth on an old garment; for the patch pulls away from the garment, and a worse tear results. [17] Nor do people put new wine

into old wineskins; otherwise the wineskins burst, and the wine pours out and the wineskins are ruined; but they put new wine into fresh wineskins, and both are preserved."
- Matthew 9:14-17

Questions arise as to why John's disciples like John and the Pharisees fast, and Jesus' disciples don't. The Pharisees fasted on a regular basis as part of their religious practice (much of which was hypocritical). John and his disciples fasted partly because of their conditioning by the Pharisees, and partly because their leader, John, was an ascetic (he ate honey, locusts and did not drink any wine); also John was in prison, and they prayed and fasted for his release.

Jesus responds with two examples:

1. Jesus' appearance is one of joy

The king of the kingdom has come and like the appearance of the bridegroom at a wedding, it is a time for feasting, not fasting. When He is killed, then there will be reason to fast.

2. The patch and the wineskin

As I said, the reason that the Pharisee's disciples fasted was because it was imposed on them by their rules and traditions. The reason John's disciples fasted was because of the example of John and the fact that he was imprisoned.

Jesus did not lay this condition upon His disciples. He was with them so they rejoiced in his presence—no need to fast. The passage about the patch and wineskin refer to their spiritual condition. He doesn't reveal to them (like He did for His disciples – who were the new garment, new wineskin) the details of His death and resurrection because they don't believe. He was the new patch and they in their disbelief were the old cloth. He was the new wine and they in their disbelief were the old wineskins. His reproof has nothing to do with age and everything to do with faith. Jesus is warning them that their rejection of Him would ultimately cause their own demise.

Miracles

7. Official's daughter

> [18] While He was saying these things to them, a synagogue official came and bowed down before Him, and said, "My daughter has just died; but come and lay Your hand on her, and she will live." [19] Jesus got up and began to follow him, and so did His disciples.
> ...
> [23] When Jesus came into the official's house, and saw the flute-players and the crowd in noisy disorder, [24] He said, "Leave; for the girl has not died, but is asleep." And they began laughing at Him. [25] But when the crowd had been sent out, He entered and took her by the hand, and the girl got up. [26] This news spread throughout all that land.
> - Matthew 9:18-19; 23-26

The official asks Jesus to save his dying daughter. The Lord arrives after the child has died. He resurrects her from dead. This miracle prefigures His own resurrection. If He can raise her, He can also be raised.

8. Woman with hemorrhage

[19] Jesus got up and began to follow him, and so did His disciples.

[20] And a woman who had been suffering from a hemorrhage for twelve years, came up behind Him and touched the fringe of His cloak; [21] for she was saying to herself, "If I only touch His garment, I will get well." [22] But Jesus turning and seeing her said, "Daughter, take courage; your faith has made you well." At once the woman was made well.
- Matthew 9:19-22

The woman touches his cloak hoping to be healed. Jesus knows her purpose, presence and the power coming from Him (miracles in themselves). She confesses her need and thus her faith. She was revealed because it was necessary for her to know:

- How she was saved: Faith
- Who saved her: Jesus
- Why she was saved: Jesus' love
- Others had to know of her healing for God to be glorified and her re-entry into society.

9. Blind men

[27] As Jesus went on from there, two blind men followed Him, crying out, "Have mercy on us, Son of David!" [28] When He entered the house, the blind men came up to Him, and Jesus said to them, "Do you believe that I am able to do this?" They said to Him, "Yes, Lord." [29] Then He touched their eyes, saying, "It shall be done

to you according to your faith." ³⁰ And their eyes were opened. And Jesus sternly warned them: "See that no one knows about this!" ³¹ But they went out and spread the news about Him throughout all that land.
- Matthew 9:27-31

They asked for help. He confirmed their faith by healing them. They spread the news against His request. He did not want to stir up the masses before His "time" because this would limit His movements and ministry.

10. Dumb and demon-possessed

³² As they were going out, a mute, demon-possessed man was brought to Him. ³³ After the demon was cast out, the mute man spoke; and the crowds were amazed, and were saying, "Nothing like this has ever been seen in Israel." ³⁴ But the Pharisees were saying, "He casts out the demons by the ruler of the demons."
- Matthew 9:32-24

The man is brought to Jesus for healing. The performing of miracles was not a new phenomenon among the Jews. Many prophets and servants of God had performed great miracles in the past. The crowds marveled, however, because the healing of the blind and dumb man had never been done before. The Pharisees begin to accuse Him of being of Satan. (This shows how depraved they had become.)

Summary

³⁵ Jesus was going through all the cities and villages, teaching in their synagogues and proclaiming the gospel of the kingdom, and healing every kind of

> disease and every kind of sickness. [36] Seeing the people, He felt compassion for them, because they were distressed and dispirited like sheep without a shepherd. [37] Then He said to His disciples, "The harvest is plentiful, but the workers are few. [38] Therefore beseech the Lord of the harvest to send out workers into His harvest."
> - Matthew 9:35-38

Jesus, Lord of harvests

Matthew summarizes Jesus' ongoing ministry as one of teaching, preaching and healing. Jesus' teaching and call to discipleship are followed by a prayer for a response and the selection of and sending out of disciples to multiply the teaching, preaching and miracles done by Jesus.

We have, through Matthew's eyes and pen, a description of the every day life of the King, as He goes about establishing His kingdom in the hearts of men and women through His miraculous power and His inspired teaching.

CHAPTER 5
THE KINGDOM IN CONFLICT

MATTHEW 10:1-42

We are studying the person of Jesus in the book of Matthew where the gospel writer emphasizes Jesus' royalty over other aspects of His character and ministry. So far he has shown Jesus:

- As He was worshiped as king by the wise men.

- Seen as a threat by the evil king Herod.

- Shown as Lord over both Satan and the angels by defeating one and being ministered to by the others.

- Heard the King describe the nature and experience of His kingdom as He explains it in the Sermon on the Mount.

- Observed the King as He went about establishing His will (or kingdom) in the hearts of the people through His teaching and mighty miracles.

- Watched as Jesus, the King, through His teaching and miracles, call those around Him into His kingdom to become disciples.

We will now examine the natural progression of the King's work on behalf of the kingdom—and that is to prepare and send out His disciples to go and preach the good news about the kingdom and invite others to enter in.

The title of this chapter is "Kingdom in Conflict," and the reason for this is that so far there has been no opposition to the Lord and His preaching; the initial beginnings of bringing people into the kingdom has been joyful and peaceful. But with the sending out of disciples to preach the message that forces people to choose to come in or remain out of the kingdom—opposition to the disciples, the Kingdom and its King were sure to follow.

In the section covered in this chapter we will see Jesus preparing His messengers of the kingdom for the conflicts they will face.

Granting of Power

Matthew assumes that the readers know the twelve special disciples of Jesus (He had many disciples and sent out more than twelve with power, Luke 10:4-20); however this section deals specifically with the sending out of the twelve who were to become the chosen Apostles. Jesus gives them authority:

- The term denotes both power and the right to use it.

- This also demonstrates Jesus' deity as one with the ability to give spiritual power to another.

Their power is over the spiritual realm (they cast out demons) and physical world (they heal sickness and disease).

Names of Apostles

> [2] Now the names of the twelve apostles are these: The first, Simon, who is called Peter, and Andrew his brother; and James the son of Zebedee, and John his brother; [3] Philip and Bartholomew; Thomas and Matthew the tax collector; James the son of Alphaeus, and Thaddaeus; [4] Simon the Zealot, and Judas Iscariot, the one who betrayed Him.
> - Matthew 10:2-4

The term apostles means more than just a servant sent to deliver a message; it denotes a fully empowered representative or legate who acts for his lord or king. Sometimes the word is used to refer to those who helped the Apostles (Barnabas), but when referred to as the "12 Apostles" the Bible speaks of these special messages through whom:

1. The eyewitness account of the life, death and resurrection of Jesus was first proclaimed with power.

2. The ones through whom the church was established.

3. The ones through whom Jesus' instruction and teachings were recorded or confirmed for future generations.

There were 14 in all. Judas was replaced by Matthias, and Paul was called as an Apostle to the Gentiles. There will never be any others like these.

- The list is grouped in pairs (Peter always first, Judas last).
- It gives Peter's Jewish name (Simon).
- Andrew, Peter's brother, is listed with him.
- James and John, another set of brothers, are named.
- Philip and Bartholomew (Nathaniel).
- Thomas (the doubter) and Matthew (the Publican).
- Second James and Thaddeus (Lebbeus/Judas his other names).
- Second Simon (from Canaan) a zealot (member of group wanting to overthrow Roman rule).
- Judas is named last. Iscariot refers to Kerioth his home town in Judea. He was designated the traitor.

Some names are found in other lists with some changed around, however, Peter is always named first, and Judas last.

Instructions Concerning Their Mission

Their instructions not only contain information pertaining to their immediate mission in Galilee but also a wider view of their ministry to the world. Jesus prepares them in describing how they and their message would be received and what their own reaction should be to those who would accept or reject the gospel.

Ministry to Israel

> [5] These twelve Jesus sent out after instructing them: "Do not go in the way of the Gentiles, and do not enter any city of the Samaritans; [6] but rather go to the lost sheep of the house of Israel. [7] And as you go, preach, saying, 'The kingdom of heaven is at hand.' [8] Heal the sick, raise the dead, cleanse the lepers, cast out demons. Freely you received, freely give. [9] Do not acquire gold, or silver, or copper for your money belts, [10] or a bag for your journey, or even two coats, or sandals, or a staff; for the worker is worthy of his support.
> - Matthew 10:5-10

Jesus begins by giving them instructions concerning their immediate ministry to the Jews.

1. Go only to the Jews, not the Gentiles or Samaritans
(vs. 5-6)

The gospel and kingdom were to be established first among Jews and then to spread to all parts of the world (Acts 1:8; Romans. 1:16). This is what Old Testament prophecy said about the ministry of the Messiah (Joel 2:28-32).

2. Preach that the kingdom of heaven is at hand
(vs. 7)

This was to be the theme of their proclamation. The idea was that the rule of grace and the power and promises of God made to them in the Old Testament were about to be fulfilled. Their true king was to be revealed. They were continuing the message of John the Baptist because Jesus had not yet died and resurrected.

3. Power to perform miracles (vs. 8)

They were empowered to heal the sick, raise the dead and cast out demons. They received this ability for free and were to use it for the benefit of the people for free. This power would confirm the word and show Jesus' authority. (He gave them the power.)

4. What to bring and what not to bring (vs. 9-10)

They were to bring no money, no luggage, no extra clothing, shoes or staffs. They were to go as they were. Jesus sends them out with the bare physical necessities and assures them that, as His workers, He will provide for them on their journey. The King had the power and resources to provide for their work on His behalf.

Method of Operation

> [11] And whatever city or village you enter, inquire who is worthy in it, and stay at his house until you leave that city. [12] As you enter the house, give it your greeting. [13] If the house is worthy, give it your blessing of peace. But if it is not worthy, take back your blessing of peace.
> [14] Whoever does not receive you, nor heed your words, as you go out of that house or that city, shake the dust off your feet. [15] Truly I say to you, it will be more tolerable for the land of Sodom and Gomorrah in the day of judgment than for that city
> - Matthew 10:11-15

They are to preach and do their works and determine by the response of the people who are willing to accommodate them (vs. 9). When they are allowed a place to stay, they are to stay put until it is time to leave (no begging, no hopping from place to place to secure better lodging).

When they enter a house they are to offer a greeting of peace, and if the hosts are receptive of Christ, this blessing will remain upon the home; if not, the Apostles will leave and the blessing will return to them (vs. 12-13).

If this occurs, they are to leave and as a sign that they have been there and been rejected they are to shake the dust of that place off of themselves as a sign of the rejection that they have suffered (vs. 14). Jesus reminds them of the judgment reserved for those who reject or shake off their message (vs. 15).

Warning as to the Response of the People

Here Jesus warns them about the response they will receive not only from the Jews but also from the Gentiles as they bring the gospel beyond Israel after He's gone. This is a warning of the conflict to come.

1. People will not take happily to the message

> [16] "Behold, I send you out as sheep in the midst of wolves; so be shrewd as serpents and innocent as doves. [17] But beware of men, for they will hand you over to the courts and scourge you in their synagogues; [18] and you will even be brought before governors and kings for My sake, as a testimony to them and to the Gentiles.
> - Matthew 10:16-18

He explains the true nature of the world (sheep and wolves) and the need to be harmless. They will be, in some cases, brought before lower (Jews) or higher (governors, kings) leaders because of the gospel. In doing so they will cause even the leaders to hear and examine the message of Christ.

2. Jesus will provide in their hour of trial

> [19] But when they hand you over, do not worry about how or what you are to say; for it will be given you in that hour what you are to say. [20] For it is not you who speak, but it is the Spirit of your Father who speaks in you.
> - Matthew 10:19-20

Jesus is not promising to protect them against imprisonment, torture or even death (which all except John suffered). He promises to inspire them in their proclamation and defense of the gospel through the Holy Spirit when the time comes. They may be persecuted but they will not be confused when their time to speak up comes.

3. Results of their preaching

> [21] "Brother will betray brother to death, and a father his child; and children will rise up against parents and cause them to be put to death. [22] You will be hated by all because of My name, but it is the one who has endured to the end who will be saved.
> [23] "But whenever they persecute you in one city, flee to the next; for truly I say to you, you will not finish going through the cities of Israel until the Son of Man comes.
> - Matthew 10:21-23

The gospel will bring division within families. They will be persecuted because of the message they bring and the result it causes. Only those who persevere will be saved. It is not the call to apostleship that saves them, but faithfulness (despite persecution) to the end that saves them, just as perseverance saves us. He prophesies that the destruction of the Jewish nation (70 AD/Rome) will occur before they will be able to bring the news to all towns. (The term "Son of Man" refers to judgment and in this case a judgment upon the Jews.)

Instructions on Their Response to the People's Reaction to the Gospel

1. Don't be surprised

> [24] "A disciple is not above his teacher, nor a slave above his master. [25] It is enough for the disciple that he become like his teacher, and the slave like his master. If they have called the head of the house Beelzebul, how much more will they malign the members of his household!
> - Matthew 10:24-25

Don't be surprised if they treat you as they do Me. If they accused Him of being the Devil, imagine what they will say of His followers?

2. Don't be afraid

> [26] "Therefore do not fear them, for there is nothing concealed that will not be revealed, or hidden that will not be known. [27] What I tell you in the darkness, speak

in the light; and what you hear whispered in your ear, proclaim upon the housetops. [28] Do not fear those who kill the body but are unable to kill the soul; but rather fear Him who is able to destroy both soul and body in hell. [29] Are not two sparrows sold for a cent? And yet not one of them will fall to the ground apart from your Father. [30] But the very hairs of your head are all numbered. [31] So do not fear; you are more valuable than many sparrows.

[32] "Therefore everyone who confesses Me before men, I will also confess him before My Father who is in heaven. [33] But whoever denies Me before men, I will also deny him before My Father who is in heaven.
- Matthew 10:26-33

- Of failure: everything that is secret now (their schemes and your gospel) will one day be revealed and out in the open (vs. 26-27).

- Of death: they may kill your bodies but they cannot destroy your souls which are precious in the sight of the Father (vs. 28-31).

- Of being wrong: those who confess Christ are on God's side; those who deny Christ, they are the ones who are against God (vs. 32-33).

Comment on the Reasons for the Negative Response to the Gospel

1. The gospel brings division not unity

[34] "Do not think that I came to bring peace on the earth;

> I did not come to bring peace, but a sword. [35] For I came to set a man against his father, and a daughter against her mother, and a daughter-in-law against her mother-in-law; [36] and a man's enemies will be the members of his household.
> - Matthew 10:34-36

The gospel brings peace between God and man and promotes peace among brethren, but creates a natural dividing line between those who accept it and those who reject it.

2. The gospel demands the highest loyalty

> [37] "He who loves father or mother more than Me is not worthy of Me; and he who loves son or daughter more than Me is not worthy of Me. [38] And he who does not take his cross and follow after Me is not worthy of Me. [39] He who has found his life will lose it, and he who has lost his life for My sake will find it.
> - Matthew 10:37-39

A loyalty that puts Christ above the closest of physical relationships, even above preservation of life itself if need be.

Jesus explains that the negative response they will encounter shouldn't surprise or frighten them because it is natural. The gospel is exclusive in nature and demands total commitment from those it calls. It is this exclusive nature of the message that creates division among nations, families, and even individuals who must wrestle with the question, "Will I abandon all, including self, to follow Jesus?"

(Exclusive in the sense that there is no other way except through Jesus Christ that one can be saved, Acts 4:12.)

Promise to those who respond

> ⁴⁰ "He who receives you receives Me, and he who receives Me receives Him who sent Me. ⁴¹ He who receives a prophet in the name of a prophet shall receive a prophet's reward; and he who receives a righteous man in the name of a righteous man shall receive a righteous man's reward. ⁴² And whoever in the name of a disciple gives to one of these little ones even a cup of cold water to drink, truly I say to you, he shall not lose his reward."
> - Matthew 10:40-42

There is a promise of reward to not only those who receive the message of Christ from the mouth of the Apostles but also those who in turn pass it along to others. Any good thing (even the smallest gesture such as a drink of water) in the name of Jesus is counted in the chain of faith and future blessings that begin with God through Christ and extend to the Apostles and everyone who believes.

This promise is not just for those who responded directly to the Apostles but for all who ultimately will respond to their message.

Summary

We see the King preparing His servants for the task at hand: to announce on His behalf the establishment of His kingdom among men (it's already established in the spiritual realm "...thy kingdom come, thy will be done on earth as it is in heaven... Matthew 6:10). He calls them, equips them with power, instructs them as to what their mission is and how to accomplish it, and ends with a warning about obstacles and an encouragement concerning their reward.

Jesus the King does the same thing today with us:

- He calls us and adds us to His kingdom (the church) through His gospel (Acts 2:37-47).
- He equips us with the Holy Spirit (Acts 2:38).
- He instructs us about our mission and strategy from His word (Matthew 28:18-20, II Timothy 3:16).
- He provides encouragement and warnings through the church and its teachers (II Thessalonians 2:17, II Timothy 4:2).

In this way the King continues to send out His servants to announce the good news of the kingdom, and the conflicts He spoke of there continue to be the ones we struggle with today. We need to remember what He told the Apostles about dealing with those conflicts.

Don't be surprised – if they treated Him badly, they will do it to His servants, even today.

Don't be afraid – He encouraged them to not be afraid concerning failure, death or being wrong. He promises us the same encouragement and assurance today.

CHAPTER 6
THE KINGDOM GROWS

MATTHEW 13:1-52

So far in our study we have seen that Matthew focuses on Jesus' royal character as the King of the kingdom of heaven. Matthew has described:

- The King Himself as Lord over the spirit world.

- The nature and experience one can find in the kingdom of the King.

- The King establishing His kingdom.

- The King preparing others to go and spread the borders of the kingdom.

In this chapter we will examine one of the basic tools that the King used in helping His kingdom to grow. Since faith is the key that allows one to enter the kingdom, the nourishing of that faith is the way that Jesus uses to promote individual growth of those already in the kingdom.

> So faith comes from hearing, and hearing by the word of Christ.
> - Romans 10:17

One of Jesus' methods for developing the faith of His disciples was His use of parables. Matthew explains that Jesus did this for two reasons:

1. To continue the teaching and maturation of those in the kingdom.
2. To keep hidden the things of the kingdom from those who disbelieved and rejected Him.

Many times He would be teaching a large crowd, and in the group would be both believers and non-believers. The parable format was perfect in reaching one group while leaving out the other. For this reason I'd like to talk about parables as a form of teaching in order to better understand the actual parables that Jesus used to teach His followers.

Parables

The word "parable" means to place beside. In the biblical context it signified the placing of two or more objects together in order to compare them. Jesus used the parable approach so He could lay physical/material things alongside the unseen spiritual things of the kingdom. When one understood the relationships, functions and lessons that the physical things taught, they then had insight into the workings of the spiritual things of the kingdom. The parable was an effective teaching tool because in it the physical things mirrored the spiritual things.

In addition to this, it was a format that was understood by those who were uneducated, and the information was easily remembered.

Most parables contained an imaginary story about something that could have happened, but was used to illustrate some higher spiritual truth. These were not fables or myths because the lessons contained stories that could have actually happened.

Parables were not a device invented by Jesus but He used this form of teaching with great insight and effect. In the New Testament only Jesus uses parables, and they are recorded in the gospels of Matthew, Mark, and Luke but not in John. Some are repeated in more than one gospel, and many are exclusive to one gospel (i.e. Pearl of Great Price – Matthew; Good Samaritan – Luke).

In order to draw accurate lessons from the parables there are some basic rules to follow:

1. Look for the spiritual truth as it applies to the situation that prompted the telling of the parable in the first place.

For example, it was the grumbling of the Pharisees who were offended that Jesus ate with sinners that prompted the telling of the parable of the Prodigal Son. In order to properly interpret the parable one must keep the conflict between the Pharisees and Jesus in mind.

2. Avoid oversimplification or complication.

For example, to say that the parable of the Good Samaritan teaches that the doing of good to others is the be all and end all of Christianity neglects to take into consideration the cross of Christ and the need for repentance and faith. This would oversimplify the meaning of this teaching.

On the other hand, if one says that the parable about the master who paid each of his workers the exact same salary for varying hours of work should be a guide to our business ethics misses the point of the parable by giving too much attention to the details of the story. This parable in Matthew 20:1-17 is about grace, not economics. One needs to search for the general spiritual principle that includes the greatest number of details.

3. Parables illustrate truth (like pictures in a textbook illustrate the text) but they do not prove truth. We shouldn't formulate doctrine based on parables alone.

For example, none of the parables prove that Jesus is the Son of God. We need to look to other passages that describe His miracles, teachings and resurrection in order to establish this important point of doctrine.

We need to understand that parables are not doctrinal statements, but they are figurative ways of pointing towards unseen things. Parables lay down a story with concrete things next to spiritual and unseen things so that through what we see what is unseen comes into view.

4. Look for the meaning or conclusion within the parable itself or within the context before drawing your own conclusion.

Sometimes Jesus gives the meaning of the parable at the beginning or at the end of the story (The Rich Fool, 12:16-21). Sometimes He asks one of His listeners to give the meaning

(The Good Samaritan, Luke 10:25-37). There are instances where He responds to a question about the parable from a listener in the group. For example, His disciples ask Him how something entering a man's mouth defiles him (Mark 7:17-23). Then there are those times when people are left to draw their own conclusions. In Mark chapter 12 the gospel writer describes the religious leaders drawing the correct conclusion from a parable about wicked servants beating and killing their master's son, was really a parable directed at them.

Usually the primary meaning is already contained within the parable itself and is applicable to the situation that the parable first addresses. For example, the parable about the Prodigal Son is first and foremost about forgiveness. Any application made from that parable begins with this idea. Correctly interpreting a parable requires us to grasp and explain this primary meaning in the story itself before making applications to modern situations. In other words we must ask ourselves, "What is the lesson for the people in the parable?" Once we have determined this we can make other comparisons and applications to situations today.

5. Jesus and His parables are one.

Other teachers and moralists can be separated from their teachings, but not Jesus. For example, Confucius, the Chinese moralist wrote many parables and sayings but these were based on ancient wisdom and practical intelligence, not on himself. Voltaire, the French philosopher wrote fables commenting on social issues and human nature, but he himself was not at the center of his own fables.

Jesus' parables, on the other hand, are about Himself and His kingdom. The reason people failed to understand His parables was because they failed to accept Him as the Messiah. They understood the story, but the significance of the parables was lost on them because they did not believe that He was the Son of God, and it was this insight that unlocked the true meaning of His parables.

He told the parables in such a way that in rejecting Him, they were unable to understand the things concerning the kingdom taught in the parables. He was the key that unlocked the hidden meanings in the stories.

"Kingdom" Parables

Many of Jesus' parables were about the kingdom, its nature, its coming and its value. Matthew's gospel has seven of these types of parables contained in chapter thirteen alone! The interpretation of these particular parables has varied throughout the years depending on the theological position one held. For example:

> [20] And again He said, "To what shall I compare the kingdom of God? [21] It is like leaven, which a woman took and hid in three pecks of flour until it was all leavened."
> - Matthew 13:20-21

1. One view sees the kingdom coming suddenly and cataclysmically in the future, therefore all parables concerning the kingdom are seen from this perspective.

2. Another view teaches that the kingdom is fully realized and completed here, and we are only adding to it as time goes by.

3. In my opinion, the view that is more biblically accurate says that the kingdom has already been established by Christ here on earth, but will be fulfilled with the resurrection and glorification of the saints when Jesus returns.

Kingdom parables are meant to demonstrate the behavior and spiritual development of kingdom dwellers until the King returns.

Parables in Matthew

In Matthew 13 we see seven kingdom parables and an explanation of the reasons for using parables, as well as examples of most of the devices concerning parables mentioned in this section of study.

> [3] And He spoke many things to them in parables, saying, "Behold, the sower went out to sow; [4] and as he sowed, some seeds fell beside the road, and the birds came and ate them up. [5] Others fell on the rocky places, where they did not have much soil; and immediately they sprang up, because they had no depth of soil. [6] But when the sun had risen, they were scorched; and because they had no root, they withered away. [7] Others fell among the thorns, and the thorns came up and choked them out. [8] And others fell on the good soil and yielded a crop, some a hundredfold, some sixty, and some thirty. [9] He who has ears, let him hear."
> - Matthew 13:3-9

Here Jesus is telling the parable of the Sower and the Seed as a response to the rejection He has experienced from the people and their leaders. The parable will teach that not all will receive the kingdom, and provides an explanation as to why He will now use parables exclusively in His teaching ministry as a way of separating believers from non-believers.

> [10] And the disciples came and said to Him, "Why do You speak to them in parables?" [11] Jesus answered them, "To you it has been granted to know the mysteries of the kingdom of heaven, but to them it has not been granted. [12] For whoever has, to him more shall be

given, and he will have an abundance; but whoever does not have, even what he has shall be taken away from him. [13] Therefore I speak to them in parables; because while seeing they do not see, and while hearing they do not hear, nor do they understand. [14] In their case the prophecy of Isaiah is being fulfilled, which says,

'You will keep on hearing, but will not understand;
You will keep on seeing, but will not perceive;
[15] For the heart of this people has become dull,
With their ears they scarcely hear,
And they have closed their eyes,
Otherwise they would see with their eyes,
Hear with their ears,
And understand with their heart and return,
And I would heal them.'

[16] But blessed are your eyes, because they see; and your ears, because they hear. [17] For truly I say to you that many prophets and righteous men desired to see what you see, and did not see it, and to hear what you hear, and did not hear it.
- Matthew 13:10-17

Verses 18-23 give us an example of Jesus explaining His teaching to the disciples as well as providing the correct commentary and meaning of the parable of the sower.

[18] "Hear then the parable of the sower. [19] When anyone hears the word of the kingdom and does not understand it, the evil one comes and snatches away what has been sown in his heart. This is the one on whom seed was sown beside the road. [20] The one on whom seed was sown on the rocky places, this is the man who hears the word and immediately receives it with joy; [21] yet he has no firm root in himself, but is only

temporary, and when affliction or persecution arises because of the word, immediately he falls away. [22] And the one on whom seed was sown among the thorns, this is the man who hears the word, and the worry of the world and the deceitfulness of wealth choke the word, and it becomes unfruitful. [23] And the one on whom seed was sown on the good soil, this is the man who hears the word and understands it; who indeed bears fruit and brings forth, some a hundredfold, some sixty, and some thirty."
- Matthew 13:18-23

The remaining kingdom parables are in groups of three, separated by two statements and followed by a summary:

A) Parables

- Wheat and Tares (vs. 24-30)
- Growing Seed (vs. 31-32)
- Leaven (vs. 33)

B) Parenthetical statement that the use of parables by the Messiah was according to prophecy about Him (vs. 34-35).

C) Explanation of the Parable of Wheat and Tares in response to a question from the disciples (vs. 36-43).

D) Parables – not all will enter the kingdom.

- Treasure (vs. 44)
- Pearl (vs. 45-46)
- Net (vs. 47-50)

E) Summary statement (vs. 51-52)

[51] "Have you understood all these things?" They said to

Him, "Yes." ⁵² And Jesus said to them, "Therefore every scribe who has become a disciple of the kingdom of heaven is like a head of a household, who brings out of his treasure things new and old."
- Matthew 13:51-52

Jesus asks if they understand the parables, and they say that they do. He responds with yet another parable. This time He compares them to the head of a household whose job it is to provide for the needs of a household.

In explaining the parable Jesus says that they are the providers of the household (kingdom) and will provide what they have been given and taught as well as what they will see and experience (their training in the kingdom). They possess some old truths such as things known and accepted (the Law and Prophets). They also have some new truths that they have learned from Jesus through the parables and witnessed with their very eyes (death, burial and resurrection of Jesus; power of the Holy Spirit).

If they have learned and understood what He has taught them, they will be able to see how both are connected and thus be able to feed and establish the kingdom accordingly.

CHAPTER 7
KINGDOM KINDNESS

MATTHEW 14:13-15:39

We are studying the royal person of Jesus as He is described by Matthew in his gospel. Matthew presents us with an image of Jesus as the King of the kingdom of heaven on earth, and in his gospel we see:

- Jesus worshiped by the wise
- Jesus, Lord even of spirits (good and bad)
- Jesus explaining His kingdom
- Jesus establishing His kingdom
- Jesus preparing kingdom workers
- Jesus helping the kingdom grow

Every time we turn to a new scene through Matthew's eyes, he reveals yet another aspect of Jesus' royal nature and work.

In these two chapters we will see some of the many acts of kindness Jesus performed on behalf of the people. Usually a king is the recipient of service, not the one doing the serving. A king has many servants and their task is to find out what he wants and then provide it for him. Matthew shows us how different the King of the kingdom of heaven is in that it is He that serves, it is He that fills the needs of His subjects. In Matthew 14 and 15, Matthew describes seven instances of the King's kindness towards others.

1. Feeding the 5000

> [13] Now when Jesus heard about John, He withdrew from there in a boat to a secluded place by Himself; and when the people heard of this, they followed Him on foot from the cities. [14] When He went ashore, He saw a large crowd, and felt compassion for them and healed their sick.
>
> [15] When it was evening, the disciples came to Him and said, "This place is desolate and the hour is already late; so send the crowds away, that they may go into the villages and buy food for themselves." [16] But Jesus said to them, "They do not need to go away; you give them something to eat!" 17 They said to Him, "We have here only five loaves and two fish." [18] And He said, "Bring them here to Me." [19] Ordering the people to sit down on the grass, He took the five loaves and the two fish, and looking up toward heaven, He blessed the food, and breaking the loaves He gave them to the disciples, and the disciples gave them to the crowds, [20] and they all ate and were satisfied. They picked up what was left over of the broken pieces, twelve full baskets. [21] There were about five thousand men who ate, besides women and children.
> - Matthew 14:13-21

Matthew gives the details of John the Baptist's execution before he describes the scene where Jesus is with the multitude. Perhaps he was trying to convey the idea that after John's death, many of his followers began to follow Jesus, and this explains the surge in the number of people seeking out the Lord for comfort and teaching.

In this scene Matthew notes that Jesus' reaction to John's death is to retreat to a remote spot probably to mourn and pray over the death of His cousin and forerunner, John. Matthew says that the people received word of where He was and followed Him.

When Jesus returns from His retreat He finds more than 5000 people awaiting Him. Matthew says that Jesus had compassion on them because they were hungry, tired and without direction or hope. He not only cared for their spiritual well being but also understood their basic needs for food and rest.

His disciples suggest that they send the people away to care for their own needs. Jesus responds that they (the disciples) care for them, and they answer that they only have five loaves and two fish. Jesus takes and multiplies these in a way that all eat sufficiently. Once distributed, the Apostles discover that there were 12 baskets of bread left over.

The point here was not the performing of a miracle to impress the crowd. Jesus used His power to provide an act of kindness towards these people. He showed the disciples that He was the source that provided for their needs as well, even if their need was to feed more than 5000 people. Jesus does the miracle as an act of kindness towards the multitude and an act of power to build the faith of His disciples.

2. Strengthening the faith of His disciples

[22] Immediately He made the disciples get into the boat and go ahead of Him to the other side, while He sent the crowds away. [23] After He had sent the crowds away, He went up on the mountain by Himself to pray; and when it was evening, He was there alone. [24] But the boat was already a long distance from the land, battered by the waves; for the wind was contrary. [25] And in the fourth watch of the night He came to them, walking on the sea. [26] When the disciples saw Him walking on the sea, they were terrified, and said, "It is a ghost!" And they cried out in fear. [27] But immediately Jesus spoke to them, saying, "Take courage, it is I; do not be afraid."

[28] Peter said to Him, "Lord, if it is You, command me to come to You on the water." [29] And He said, "Come!" And Peter got out of the boat, and walked on the water and came toward Jesus. [30] But seeing the wind, he became frightened, and beginning to sink, he cried out, "Lord, save me!" [31] Immediately Jesus stretched out His hand and took hold of him, and said to him, "You of little faith, why did you doubt?" [32] When they got into the boat, the wind stopped. [33] And those who were in the boat worshiped Him, saying, "You are certainly God's Son!"
- Matthew 14:22-33

Note that Jesus remains with the people and sends the Apostles ahead to cross back over the lake. He also retreats in order to continue His time of prayer. Matthew says that their boat was caught up in a storm, and at a critical moment Jesus appears to the frightened Apostles while walking on the water. Again, the miracle demonstrates His Lordship over the material world and the physical laws of that material world.

In the miracle of the loaves and fish, the disciples were strangely silent; they were entering a space where their sense of reality was being sorely tested. Once in the boat, however, they were once again on familiar terrain. After all, they were fishermen, and they understood the sea. They were not afraid of storms since these were a regular occurrence in the type of work that they did. However when Jesus appeared to them they were afraid to the point of crying out. The Lord comforted them with assurances that He was not a ghost nor was this a nightmare or vision.

At this point Peter decides to test what he sees and asks Jesus to let him also walk on the water. For a time his faith is solid and he succeeds. Then he realizes that this isn't a dream. The wind is real as well as the danger. The Apostle begins to doubt and that hesitation causes him to sink. Peter's faith is not strong enough to permit him to continue walking on the water, but by this point it is strong enough to ask Jesus for help, which the Lord provides.

Note that when Jesus and Peter return to the boat, the storm stops and the Apostles' collective faith is strengthened to the point where they no longer see Him simply as a teacher or prophet, but worship Him as God.

3. Heals those in remote areas

> [34] When they had crossed over, they came to land at Gennesaret. [35] And when the men of that place recognized Him, they sent word into all that surrounding district and brought to Him all who were sick; [36] and they implored Him that they might just touch the fringe of His cloak; and as many as touched it were cured.
> - Matthew 14:34-36

There are two remarkable things about this brief passage:

1. That Jesus would even go to this very small and remote area on the northwest shore of the Sea of Galilee. One who could do miracles and spoke from God traveled to this backwater place to minister to the least important in the eyes of men.

2. The other remarkable thing was how He ministered to them. They brought all who were sick and these were cured without a word or a long profession of faith. They simply touched His cloak and were completely healed.

The King showed His concern for all of those in the kingdom and demonstrated the fact that His power was available to all who came to Him. No matter how poor or how remote, all had access to the King.

4. Jesus lifts a heavy burden

Jewish life, especially for the common person, was not easy in Jesus' day. Their tiny nation was under the imperial thumb of the pagan Roman Empire. They had dangerous regional enemies to the north and south. Their own political leaders were cruel and murderous. To make matters worse, their religious leaders had so complicated their religion that it had become nearly impossible to practice it with a clear conscience.

One of their man-made religious practices was the issue of being "clean or unclean" for purposes of worship. The Law of Moses had certain prescriptions about purification rites to be performed if one had a disease or had touched a dead animal or person. These usually involved a cleansing and quarantine of some kind followed by an offering at the temple to signal that a person was ready to re-enter the social and religious life of the community.

To these laws the Jewish teachers had added all kinds of conditions and ceremonies. One of these was the meticulous washing of hands and dishes required even if a person had touched any object that may have been touched by a non-Jew. This was far beyond what God intended and made the common man's life very complicated in his effort to serve the Lord. This is the point Jesus addresses in 15:1-9.

> [1] Then some Pharisees and scribes came to Jesus from Jerusalem and said, [2] "Why do Your disciples break the tradition of the elders? For they do not wash their hands when they eat bread." [3] And He answered and said to them, "Why do you yourselves transgress the commandment of God for the sake of your tradition? [4] For God said, 'Honor your father and mother,' and, 'He who speaks evil of father or mother is to be put to death.' [5] But you say, 'Whoever says to his father or mother, "Whatever I have that would help you has been given to God," [6] he is not to honor his father or his mother.' And by this you invalidated the word of God for the sake of your tradition. [7] You hypocrites, rightly did Isaiah prophesy of you:
>
> [8] 'This people honors Me with their lips,
> But their heart is far away from Me.
> [9] 'But in vain do they worship Me,
> Teaching as doctrines the precepts of men.'"
> - Matthew 15:1-9

In this passage Jesus reveals the double standard that the Jewish leaders lived by in their own lives. They created these burdensome laws without God's consent. They twisted God's legitimate commands in order to suit themselves. For example:

- They would pledge to the temple the money that would normally be used to help their parents which was a legitimate duty of children towards fathers and mothers.

- By pledging this money they would, in effect, freeze their assets. Once their parents had died, they would reclaim their pledge from the temple for their personal use once again.

Jesus reveals this hypocrisy, and in doing so stripped these people of the moral authority they used to lord their will over the people.

[10] After Jesus called the crowd to Him, He said to them, "Hear and understand. [11] It is not what enters into the mouth that defiles the man, but what proceeds out of the mouth, this defiles the man."

[12] Then the disciples came and said to Him, "Do You know that the Pharisees were offended when they heard this statement?" [13] But He answered and said, "Every plant which My heavenly Father did not plant shall be uprooted. [14] Let them alone; they are blind guides of the blind. And if a blind man guides a blind man, both will fall into a pit."

[15] Peter said to Him, "Explain the parable to us." [16] Jesus said, "Are you still lacking in understanding also? [17] Do you not understand that everything that goes into the mouth passes into the stomach, and is eliminated? [18] But the things that proceed out of the mouth come from the heart, and those defile the man. [19] For out of the heart come evil thoughts, murders, adulteries, fornications, thefts, false witness, slanders. [20] These are the things which defile the man; but to eat with unwashed hands does not defile the man."
- Matthew 15:10-20

This is a continuation of the process of lifting heavy burdens from the people. Jesus explains that we become impure (defiled/not worthy for worship) by what comes from our hearts and out of our mouths, not by what goes into our stomachs. He explains that it is our words, thoughts and evil intentions that make us unworthy, not what we eat.

Of course, the disciples realized the trouble this was going to cause with the Pharisees who oversaw and taught extensively on the subject of food laws. Jesus is effectively abolishing these for those in His kingdom. He is the guide who sees, they are the blind ones. Even though the teaching is radical, He leaves His followers to choose which leader/guide they will follow.

Again, Peter is the one who needs and seeks clarification on this matter. Jesus explains why food itself cannot contaminate the soul. Sin defiles, not food.

What a heavy burden is lifted here, but only for those in the kingdom. It relieves one burden but adds another: the burden of persecution for those who will follow Jesus as guide.

5. Kindness towards the Gentiles

> [21] Jesus went away from there, and withdrew into the district of Tyre and Sidon. [22] And a Canaanite woman from that region came out and began to cry out, saying, "Have mercy on me, Lord, Son of David; my daughter is cruelly demon-possessed." [23] But He did not answer her a word. And His disciples came and implored Him, saying, "Send her away, because she keeps shouting at us." [24] But He answered and said, "I was sent only to the lost sheep of the house of Israel." [25] But she came and began to bow down before Him, saying, "Lord, help me!"

> [26] And He answered and said, "It is not good to take the children's bread and throw it to the dogs." [27] But she said, "Yes, Lord; but even the dogs feed on the crumbs which fall from their masters' table." [28] Then Jesus said to her, "O woman, your faith is great; it shall be done for you as you wish." And her daughter was healed at once.
> - Matthew 15:21-28

Some actually think that Jesus is being unkind to this woman because of His reference to dogs. His claim to feed the children first was based on the priority of His work which was to bring the good news of the kingdom to the Jews first then to the Gentiles (as this woman was). The comment about dogs looks harsh but is really quite harmless. First, we feed the children before we feed the pets. Jesus was stating a matter of order, not that others are dogs.

Again, the true kindness is that Jesus defies social convention (He has a conversation with a woman); He defies national prejudice (He converses with a Gentile); He alters His timetable (healing a Gentile before the time for bringing them the gospel is at hand); and all of these acts of kindness done towards those in need.

6. Kindness towards the needy

> [29] Departing from there, Jesus went along by the Sea of Galilee, and having gone up on the mountain, He was sitting there. [30] And large crowds came to Him, bringing with them those who were lame, crippled, blind, mute, and many others, and they laid them down at His feet; and He healed them. [31] So the crowd marveled as they saw the mute speaking, the crippled restored, and the lame walking, and the blind seeing; and they glorified the God of Israel.

- Matthew 15:29-31

This is a repetition of the scene that took place in Gennesaret where Jesus heals many. In this instance the diseases and infirmities are described:

- Not just general illness but conditions that normally had no improvement or cure.
- Blindness, deafness, those with severe handicaps were restored.

Again, there is no teaching accompanying these miracles. They were done to relieve the pain and suffering of the people of that area.

This kindness had its effect on people in that God was glorified, just as Jesus said that He would be when good works were done in His name.

7. Kindness for its own sake

[32] And Jesus called His disciples to Him, and said, "I feel compassion for the people, because they have remained with Me now three days and have nothing to eat; and I do not want to send them away hungry, for they might faint on the way." [33] The disciples said to Him, "Where would we get so many loaves in this desolate place to satisfy such a large crowd?" [34] And Jesus said to them, "How many loaves do you have?" And they said, "Seven, and a few small fish." [35] And He directed the people to sit down on the ground; [36] and He took the seven loaves and the fish; and giving thanks, He broke them and started giving them to the disciples, and the disciples gave them to the people. [37] And they all ate and were satisfied, and they picked up what was

left over of the broken pieces, seven large baskets full. ³⁸ And those who ate were four thousand men, besides women and children.

³⁹ And sending away the crowds, Jesus got into the boat and came to the region of Magadan.
- Matthew 15:32-39

Matthew completes this sequence with a second instance where Jesus miraculously feeds a large multitude of people. His ministry of healing has drawn great multitudes and now that they are here they need to be fed before Jesus sends them away so He can move on to another place. He approaches the disciples with the problem and again they respond with doubt. He performs a miracle similar to the previous one and provides food for the large crowd.

This is one further attempt to show them not only His power but also the fact that His power is in the service of His mercy and kindness towards those in need.

Summary

Matthew shows us a facet of the King's character that is very comforting to those in the kingdom: His kindness. His power over the spirits, the material world and mankind in general is enough to intimidate us into His kingdom, but not very comforting. Matthew, in showing us His great kindness, makes our submission to the King something we don't have to worry or be afraid of because in the kingdom there is mercy.

It is His absolute power that draws people to the King and His kingdom, but it is His kindness that convinces them to stay.

The same parallel can be made for the kingdom or church today. It is the power of the gospel and the many good works in His name that bring people into the church. However, it is the love among the brethren that convinces them to stay faithful to the Lord, not the threats of punishment.

CHAPTER 8
WHO IS THE KING?

MATTHEW 16:1-28

We are studying Matthew's gospel and especially how Matthew depicts Jesus as the King of the kingdom of heaven. Matthew recounts much of the same events and teachings as the other gospel writers, but in his gospel we are able to trace this particular theme. So far we have seen various ways that Matthew has referred to Jesus' royal person, but in the following section we will see Jesus actually force the issue among His disciples. In other words, He will make His Apostles come to and admit the conclusion that only He is the ruler, the King. When we last saw the Lord and His Apostles, they were in the northern part of the country near their hometowns around the Sea of Galilee. After He finishes His ministry in this area, Jesus will go south towards Jerusalem and finish His ministry there.

When He will go to Jerusalem He will:

- Teach and confront the Pharisees
- Have a triumphal entry into the city
- Pronounce a judgment on the city and prophesy concerning its future
- He will celebrate the final Passover and initiate the Lord's Supper with His Apostles
- And finally be arrested, falsely convicted, crucified, resurrected and ascend into heaven

In the meantime, while He is in safer and more familiar surroundings, Jesus will establish, especially with His Apostles, His true identity.

Jesus will also prepare them for the rejection He will suffer at the hands of the leaders and the people.

Turning Point for the King

Every story has a dramatic turning point (e.g. the plane crashes, someone is arrested, the villain is revealed, etc.). In Matthew's account, the turning point in Jesus' ministry takes place with two events:

1. Jesus is rejected by the people of His hometown

Until Jesus returned to Nazareth, there had been a very positive response to Him and His teachings. However, we know that the tide is about to turn when the people who knew Him best and had not only witnessed His teachings and miracles, but His good life as well; when these people reject Him, we know that the change for the worse has begun.

2. Herod kills John the Baptist

Herod, at the national level, believed that John was a popular prophet, knew of his connection with Jesus, but had him executed anyway. This was a clear signal to Jesus of Herod's opposition and contempt.

Faced with this level of opposition moves Jesus to step up His efforts at strengthening the Apostles' faith and understanding of who He truly was.

Ministry to His Apostles

We've looked at this material in the previous chapter looking at it in the context of His kindness, the idea that as King Jesus was a servant of those in need. But from another perspective we also see that Jesus is building the faith of His Apostles to the point where they will be assured that He is also the Lord, the Messiah, the Divine Son of God, as well as the King. We see Him doing this in a variety of ways:

His miracles for the people

The Apostles were witnesses of the tremendous miracles Jesus performed for the people who came to Him.

- Feeding the 5000
- The sick were healed simply by touching His cloak
- Healing the Canaanite woman's daughter
- Healing the lame, blind and handicapped

- Feeding another crowd of 4000

- Healing of an epileptic boy upon a father's desperate request

Despite the miracles done among them, many of these people begin to reject the Lord, but He continues to minister to them anyways and in doing so built the faith of His Apostles.

His handling of the Jewish leaders

Most were afraid of these people, but Jesus, the King, showed His authority when He dealt with them and their schemes to destroy Him. Jesus' rejection was spearheaded by the Pharisees and Priests (Sadducees) whom, despite seeing the miracles and hearing the teachings, refused to accept the conclusion that these pointed to Jesus. They wanted to discredit and destroy Jesus in order to protect their position and hide their own sinfulness:

- They did not teach with authority and twisted the Scriptures to their own advantage.

- They did not help people or provide for them; they manipulated the people in order to maintain their position.

And so, Matthew describes several instances where the king handles His accusers and enemies who are out to discredit Him:

1. Accusation of transgressing the "tradition"

[1] Then some Pharisees and scribes came to Jesus from Jerusalem and said, [2] "Why do Your disciples break the

tradition of the elders? For they do not wash their hands when they eat bread." [3] And He answered and said to them, "Why do you yourselves transgress the commandment of God for the sake of your tradition?

[4] "For God said, 'Honor your father and mother,' and, 'He who speaks evil of father or mother is to be put to death.' [5] "But you say, 'Whoever says to his father or mother, "Whatever I have that would help you has been given to God," [6] he is not to honor his father or his mother.' And by this you invalidated the word of God for the sake of your tradition. [7] "You hypocrites, rightly did Isaiah prophesy of you:

[8] 'This people honors Me with their lips,
But their heart is far away from Me.
[9] 'But in vain do they worship Me,
Teaching as doctrines the precepts of men.'"

[10] After Jesus called the crowd to Him, He said to them, "Hear and understand. [11] "It is not what enters into the mouth that defiles the man, but what proceeds out of the mouth, this defiles the man."
[12] Then the disciples came and said to Him, "Do You know that the Pharisees were offended when they heard this statement?" [13] But He answered and said, "Every plant which My heavenly Father did not plant shall be uprooted. [14] "Let them alone; they are blind guides of the blind. And if a blind man guides a blind man, both will fall into a pit."

[15] Peter said to Him, "Explain the parable to us."

[16] Jesus said, "Are you still lacking in understanding also? [17] "Do you not understand that everything that goes into the mouth passes into the stomach, and is eliminated? [18] "But the things that proceed out of the mouth come from the heart, and those defile the man.

¹⁹ "For out of the heart come evil thoughts, murders, adulteries, fornications, thefts, false witness, slanders. ²⁰ "These are the things which defile the man; but to eat with unwashed hands does not defile the man."
- Matthew 15:1-20

We examined this episode previously and noted that Pharisees from Jerusalem (who had more authority than local scribes) came to Galilee and accused Jesus of violating the "tradition" concerning the washing of hands before eating. Now the "tradition" or "HALACHA" was the set of (631) rules set as a fence around the Law by rabbis in order to make sure one did not break the Law. It included all kinds of rituals, procedures and rules that were conceived and enforced by religious leaders without any authority from Scripture.

The Law of Moses required no inter-marrying or worship with Gentiles. These rabbis had extended this to include a rule where if you even touched something that had been previously touched by a Gentile, you were considered "unclean" or "defiled" and unable to worship without a long process of washings and rituals to correct the situation. When referring to these rules Jesus explained that a person defiles himself when he speaks evil things and does evil things that begin in his heart. What comes from the heart, Jesus taught, this is the evil that defiles a man. What he touches or eats, this has no power to defile a person.

In saying this, Jesus implied that it was the Pharisees who were impure because of their teachings and conduct that did not find a basis in the word of God.

2. The Pharisees ask for a sign

¹ The Pharisees and Sadducees came up, and testing Jesus, they asked Him to show them a sign from

heaven. ² But He replied to them, "When it is evening, you say, 'It will be fair weather, for the sky is red.' ³ "And in the morning, 'There will be a storm today, for the sky is red and threatening.' Do you know how to discern the appearance of the sky, but cannot discern the signs of the times? ⁴ "An evil and adulterous generation seeks after a sign; and a sign will not be given it, except the sign of Jonah." And He left them and went away.

⁵ And the disciples came to the other side of the sea, but they had forgotten to bring any bread. ⁶ And Jesus said to them, "Watch out and beware of the leaven of the Pharisees and Sadducees." ⁷ They began to discuss this among themselves, saying, "He said that because we did not bring any bread." ⁸ But Jesus, aware of this, said, "You men of little faith, why do you discuss among yourselves that you have no bread? ⁹ Do you not yet understand or remember the five loaves of the five thousand, and how many baskets full you picked up? ¹⁰ Or the seven loaves of the four thousand, and how many large baskets full you picked up? ¹¹ How is it that you do not understand that I did not speak to you concerning bread? But beware of the leaven of the Pharisees and Sadducees." ¹² Then they understood that He did not say to beware of the leaven of bread, but of the teaching of the Pharisees and Sadducees.
- Matthew 16:1-12

This is not the first time these leaders ask for a sign, they had done this before. They wanted a demonstration of His power or a special sign or signal for themselves. Their implication being that what He had done so far was not enough to convince them. Jesus responds by condemning their request because:

- It is an example of disbelief and an evil heart.

- It is not a sincere request based on a desire to know and believe (like Thomas' was), but a challenge born of cynicism.

Jesus knows their hearts and tells them what sign to look for: the sign of Jonah. The sign of Jonah (who was three days in the belly of the great fish and then returned) was the sign of the resurrection. The prophets said that the true sign of the legitimate Messiah would be His resurrection (Acts 2:31-32; Romans 1:1-4); they were to look for that.

In handling these men, the King prepares His disciples not only by building their faith in Him but also by showing them who will be their enemies in the future.

Miracles Performed for the Apostles

In building their faith, Jesus performed miracles for the masses and responded to the Jewish leaders who were trying to destroy His credibility and formulate a charge in order to execute Him. But Jesus also used His power in a very personal way in allowing His Apostles to see His divine and royal attributes from very close up. This He did through miracles only the Apostles were witness to:

1. Walking on water

> [22] Immediately He made the disciples get into the boat and go ahead of Him to the other side, while He sent the crowds away. [23] After He had sent the crowds away, He went up on the mountain by Himself to pray; and when it was evening, He was there alone. [24] But the boat was already a long distance from the land, battered by the waves; for the wind was contrary. [25] And in the fourth watch of the night He came to them, walking on the sea. [26] When the disciples saw Him

walking on the sea, they were terrified, and said, "It is a ghost!" And they cried out in fear. ²⁷ But immediately Jesus spoke to them, saying, "Take courage, it is I; do not be afraid."

²⁸ Peter said to Him, "Lord, if it is You, command me to come to You on the water." ²⁹ And He said, "Come!" And Peter got out of the boat, and walked on the water and came toward Jesus. ³⁰ But seeing the wind, he became frightened, and beginning to sink, he cried out, "Lord, save me!" ³¹ Immediately Jesus stretched out His hand and took hold of him, and said to him, "You of little faith, why did you doubt?" ³² When they got into the boat, the wind stopped. ³³ And those who were in the boat worshiped Him, saying, "You are certainly God's Son!"
- Matthew 14:22-33

We looked at this miracle in a previous section where Jesus comes to His Apostles who are in a boat rowing against a storm. They are afraid at first, but Peter comes out and for a while he too walks on water before doubting and needing Jesus to save him from sinking.

In the end, this miracle leads all the Apostles to worship and declare Jesus as the divine Lord, a level of faith they had not yet reached before this episode.

2. The Transfiguration

¹ Six days later Jesus took with Him Peter and James and John his brother, and led them up on a high mountain by themselves. ² And He was transfigured before them; and His face shone like the sun, and His garments became as white as light. ³ And behold, Moses and Elijah appeared to them, talking with Him.

[4] Peter said to Jesus, "Lord, it is good for us to be here; if You wish, I will make three tabernacles here, one for You, and one for Moses, and one for Elijah." [5] While he was still speaking, a bright cloud overshadowed them, and behold, a voice out of the cloud said, "This is My beloved Son, with whom I am well-pleased; listen to Him!" [6] When the disciples heard this, they fell face down to the ground and were terrified. [7] And Jesus came to them and touched them and said, "Get up, and do not be afraid." [8] And lifting up their eyes, they saw no one except Jesus Himself alone.
- Matthew 17:1-8

Peter, James and John witness the visual brightness of Jesus' divine nature and His ability to communicate beyond both the time and physical dimensions. He speaks with Moses and Elijah (who provide by their appearance a confirmation from the Law and the Prophets who Jesus really is). Luke writes that the three discussed Jesus' crucifixion. The voice from heaven also confirms Jesus' role as one who fulfills all prophecy and Law.

The instruction to, "...hear Him..." is to listen to Jesus as the final authority and final word of Law and Prophecy. He fulfills and supersedes these two.

3. The coin in the fish

[24] When they came to Capernaum, those who collected the two-drachma tax came to Peter and said, "Does your teacher not pay the two-drachma tax?" [25] He said, "Yes." And when he came into the house, Jesus spoke to him first, saying, "What do you think, Simon? From whom do the kings of the earth collect customs or poll-tax, from their sons or from strangers?" [26] When Peter said, "From strangers," Jesus said to him, "Then the

sons are exempt. [27] "However, so that we do not offend them, go to the sea and throw in a hook, and take the first fish that comes up; and when you open its mouth, you will find a shekel. Take that and give it to them for you and Me."
- Matthew 17:24-27

Peter is questioned to see if he pays the temple tax or not. Jesus tells Peter to go fish and explains that when he does so, he will find a coin in the fish's mouth with which he will pay the tax for both of them. The idea here is that it was ridiculous for Jesus, the Son of God/the King of Kings, to pay tax on His own temple. But to avoid offending those weak in the faith He instructs Peter to pay it, but with a coin obtained in a miraculous way. Of course those who didn't believe or didn't accept Jesus only saw a young teacher pay His dues.

The Apostles, however, receive yet another demonstration of Jesus' power to bolster their faith and understanding of who He was.

Special Teaching

Finally, Jesus used many opportunities to privately teach His Apostles about His role and position—teaching that the masses were not exposed to:

1. The lesson about pure and impure (Matthew 15:15-20)

After chastising the Pharisees about their hypocrisy concerning their traditions, Jesus explained privately to the Apostles why food did not defile.

This insight gave them the moral authority to refute the Jewish leaders later on.

2. Warning against the Pharisees (Matthew 16:1-12)

We read about this in Jesus' answer to the Pharisees when they requested a sign. After this incident, when Jesus was alone with the Apostles, He uses this incident to warn them about these men.

Jesus, in pointing to His miraculous feeding of the 4000 and then to the work of the Pharisees is, in effect, asking His Apostles to compare the two and realize who has the real power and authority: the Pharisees or the King of the kingdom.

3. Jesus' response to Peter's confession

> [13] Now when Jesus came into the district of Caesarea Philippi, He was asking His disciples, "Who do people say that the Son of Man is?" [14] And they said, "Some say John the Baptist; and others, Elijah; but still others, Jeremiah, or one of the prophets." [15] He said to them, "But who do you say that I am?" [16] Simon Peter answered, "You are the Christ, the Son of the living God." [17] And Jesus said to him, "Blessed are you, Simon Barjona, because flesh and blood did not reveal this to you, but My Father who is in heaven. [18] I also say to you that you are Peter, and upon this rock I will build My church; and the gates of Hades will not overpower it. [19] I will give you the keys of the kingdom of heaven; and whatever you bind on earth shall have been bound in heaven, and whatever you loose on earth shall have been loosed in heaven." [20] Then He warned the disciples that they should tell no one that He was the

Christ.
- Matthew 16:13-20

We see another climactic moment here. The miracles, responses to the leaders and special teaching they have witnessed and received have built their faith to the point where, upon being asked, Peter confesses his true and perfect belief.

Speaking ahead of the others, he declares in clear and unmistakable language what the parables, miracles and teachings were all pointing to from the very beginning:

- That Jesus is the divine Messiah.
- The King is recognized for who He is.

At this point however, Jesus teaches them beyond the point of a simple confession of faith. He teaches them that:

A) Without revelation of the Son through teachings and miracles, Peter would have never known this. Human wisdom cannot discern God's will and plan without revelation from God Himself. This is why the gospel is powerful; it reveals the will of God, which is salvation through faith in Christ.

B) Simon, the old man, the man Jesus originally called to follow Him, is truly a blessed person because of the confession he has just made.

C) Peter, the new man (rockman), will be stronger and better because of this confession. (Simon=stone; Peter=boulder/cliff)

D) This revelation which Peter has formally declared in his confession of faith will be the basis or the "rock" upon which Jesus will build His church (the called out). Now, if Jesus wanted to say that He was to build His church upon Peter, the construction of the sentence would have been, "...and upon thee, I will build my church." But the rock upon which the indestructible church was to be built was the reality and fact that Jesus is the divine Messiah, not just the acknowledgement of that fact. The church is built upon a person (Jesus) not just a doctrine (who we say He is).

E) Jesus continues to teach them further by revealing the ministry they will have:

- The "keys of the kingdom" represents the authority they will have to open the doors of the heavenly kingdom because they will possess and proclaim the gospel message and through it will bestow forgiveness of sins, the Holy Spirit and eternal life with God in heaven upon all who will believe and respond to the gospel in faith expressed through repentance and baptism (Acts 2:37- 42). The imagery of keys comes from Isaiah and David: key to the throne = authority.

- "Binding and loosening" is the authority to speak to men on behalf of God. Through the guidance of the Holy Spirit the Apostles recorded the inspired writings, which explain the gospel and define the Christian life.

It wasn't their authority, it was the authority of the word which God spoke through them.

This further teaching as a response to Peter's confession solidifies Jesus' rule as King over His kingdom and the future tasks and authority given those who will serve in His kingdom.

Prophecy Concerning the Crucifixion

One last method of teaching that Jesus used to build faith and prepare His Apostles was the giving of various prophecies concerning His death and resurrection. The prophets wrote that the single most important sign of the true Messiah was to be His resurrection, not His miracles or teachings (Isaiah 53:5-11; Psalm 16:10).

To prepare them for this last and greatest proof of His person, Jesus prophesied no less than three times (in Matthew) about His eventual death and subsequent resurrection (Matthew 16:21-28; 17:9-13; 17:22-23). This was done not only for them but also for our instruction because with these prophecies Jesus taught both them and us several important lessons about Himself specifically, and discipleship in general:

1. For Christ and His followers, death would come, but would be followed by a glorious resurrection (Matthew 16:21).

2. The cost of salvation for Him and discipleship for us is high (Matthew 16:24-26).

3. All of this: His resurrection as well as ours, was according to God's word (Matthew 17:10).

And so, with a mixture of faith in Him as the divine Messiah, King of the kingdom of heaven, and knowledge of the suffering that this title was to cost Him, the Apostles were ready to leave the relatively safe surroundings of Galilee in order to be with the King as He traveled to the city of kings and eventually to the cross.

CHAPTER 9
THE KINGDOM'S LOSS

MATTHEW 19:16-30

In our study on Jesus, the King of the kingdom, we have worked our way through Matthew's gospel observing Jesus, the King, establishing His kingdom. We have seen how He built up his Apostles' faith to the point where they confessed Him to be the divine Messiah. We have also studied His lessons about the kingdom, who can enter and who is considered great there. So far His ministry has been on an upward trajectory.

We did see, however, that with the death of John the Baptist and His subsequent rejection by the people of His hometown at Nazareth, a definite downward spiral begins.

Background

By this time Jesus' ministry in the northern part of the country near His hometown in Galilee is completed and He prepares to travel towards Jerusalem. Matthew divides the description of these events into two sections:

1. Events that take place while He is on the way to Jerusalem.
2. Events that take place in and around the city of Jerusalem.

The general acceptance and some doubt expressed in His home region are replaced by aggressive attack and total rejection as Jesus nears the city of Jerusalem.

In the section where Jesus is traveling, Matthew describes many encounters that the Lord has with different people:

- The healing of the crowds
- The discussion with the Pharisees over divorce
- Blessing children who come to Him
- The on-going discussions with the Apostles
- The blind men receiving their sight

None of these episodes, however, are as poignant and sad as the one Jesus has with the rich young ruler.

The Rich Young Ruler

> [16] And someone came to Him and said, "Teacher, what good thing shall I do that I may obtain eternal life?"
> [17] And He said to him, "Why are you asking Me about what is good? There is only One who is good; but if you

> wish to enter into life, keep the commandments." [18] Then he said to Him, "Which ones?" And Jesus said, "YOU SHALL NOT COMMIT MURDER; YOU SHALL NOT COMMIT ADULTERY; YOU SHALL NOT STEAL; YOU SHALL NOT BEAR FALSE WITNESS; [19] HONOR YOUR FATHER AND MOTHER; and YOU SHALL LOVE YOUR NEIGHBOR AS YOURSELF." [20] The young man said to Him, "All these things I have kept; what am I still lacking?" [21] Jesus said to him, "If you wish to be complete, go and sell your possessions and give to the poor, and you will have treasure in heaven; and come, follow Me." [22] But when the young man heard this statement, he went away grieving; for he was one who owned much property.
> - Matthew 19:16-22

The title of this chapter is, "The Kingdom's Loss," because of this man. He was young, successful, pious and headed in the right direction. He was searching for the kingdom but fell short because there were certain things missing in his life. In the end he loses the thing he thought he wanted, and the kingdom loses a potential soul at this point.

The Missing Ingredients

The young ruler did not have faith

This person had good intentions but not faith, and the passage demonstrates this in several ways.

1. He doesn't recognize Jesus as the Messiah but rather as some kind of guru. By referring to Him as "Good Teacher" he gives Him a compliment but not the true recognition of His actual person and rule. Even Jesus points this out. Why refer to Him as divine (good) when you don't believe?

2. He thinks that Jesus is a man like himself; a great man, but a man nevertheless. He believes the only difference between them is the secret. If Jesus gives him the secret then he will be like Jesus, fully equal.

3. He also believes that eternal life can be obtained by a man from another man, without the intervention of God. In other words, God could tell us how to do it (tell us the secret) or explain what rules to follow, but we would do it.

The young ruler, like many today, wants the right thing and he's sincere about it but he does not see that faith in Jesus is the first ingredient necessary to obtain eternal life.

The young man did not have self-awareness

His question, response and approach showed that he did not have a proper view of himself and his true condition. When the young man asks the Lord how to obtain eternal life, Jesus responds with what the young man had been taught and had tried without success. Right here we need a little background information to understand what's going on:

We are born and created to live forever, our souls are eternal and God has programmed us to know this intuitively ("He has set eternity in their heart." Ecclesiastes 3:11).

The problem, of course, is sin. Sin is the breaking of God's laws and disobedience to His word. When we sin we are separated from God, denied our eternal life with Him, and yet our innate knowledge of our own eternal nature yearns to be reunited with Him. The sense of incompleteness, the dissatisfaction with this world, the feelings of deep guilt, fear and dread of judgment all stem from our desire to be united with God as we once were before sin.

Now there are two ways this reuniting with God, and this experience of eternal life can be accomplished.

1. Never sin in the first place. If one keeps perfectly all the commands of God and never violates His will or His word, then there is never any separation in the first place.
2. Realize that we are sinners and thus separated from God, and subject to condemnation. Thankfully accept God's gracious offer of forgiveness and restoration to unity and eternal life with Him.

Okay, now back to our story with the young ruler. The young ruler understood that if one never broke the Law they would experience eternal life and union with God.

In his mind he had done what a person had to do to gain eternal life (keep God's laws), but he wasn't experiencing the promised results: eternal life! Something was missing, something was left out, he had a missing ingredient, and he thought Jesus would supply it. The young man didn't see himself correctly. He didn't see that he was a sinner, a failure before God despite his wealth, a condemned man separated from God by sin. He thought he was innocent!

Of course intelligent, respectable, moral, successful people have always had a hard time recognizing that pride, greed, self-righteousness, worldliness, lack of faith will send you to hell as easily as murder and adultery. Model citizens need God's forgiveness just like everyone else. The Bible says that all are sinners, and stand condemned (Romans 3:23). The rich young ruler recognized that he had a deep need but did not see that his need was for salvation though the mercy and forgiveness of God offered by the very person that stood before him.

The truth was that he was a sinner who needed grace, not a saint who needed a secret.

The young man did not have a changed heart

When Jesus said to this man, "...one thing you lack..." He didn't mean that he had everything except one thing. This is what the young ruler thought; he had it all and was missing one last great secret that Jesus could give him.

In the Greek, this expression means, "you are behind one thing" or "one thing is continuously ahead of you." Jesus was saying, "despite what you have or don't have, one thing will not let you pass" (like a runner ahead of you that won't let you by). For this man, his love and dependence on wealth was the thing that wouldn't let him pass. He could have had other sins, other faults as well, but the thing that was blocking his faith, his self-awareness and his repentance was his love of money. Jesus explains to him how to overcome this sin, how to remove this obstacle: by giving to others and then giving himself to the Lord.

For some, the obstacle is drugs, sexual sin, pride, stubbornness or laziness. However for each person the solution is different in how to remove the obstacles to self-awareness and faith.

For this man, the problem was the love of and dependence on wealth. Jesus was not making the giving away of one's wealth a condition of salvation—he was removing the obstacle in this man's life so he could believe and repent, and thus be saved.

The rich young ruler wanted treasure in heaven but didn't realize that it was his attitude towards his earthly treasure that was blocking the way.

Jesus' invitation to follow Him also revealed that the young man was not only unwilling to let go of his wealth, he was also unwilling to redirect his life in order to follow Jesus, and this was the basic reason that he was denied the eternal life he so wanted.

The Kingdom's Wealth

The episode with the young ruler sets up an opportunity for Jesus to teach the Apostles about one of the great obstacles faced by those seeking to enter into the kingdom.

> [23] And Jesus said to His disciples, "Truly I say to you, it is hard for a rich man to enter the kingdom of heaven. [24] "Again I say to you, it is easier for a camel to go through the eye of a needle, than for a rich man to enter the kingdom of God." [25] When the disciples heard this, they were very astonished and said, "Then who can be saved?" [26] And looking at them Jesus said to them, "With people this is impossible, but with God all things are possible."
> - Matthew 19:23-26

Jesus warns His Apostles against worldliness, the enemy of the kingdom. The point Jesus makes is the same one He made in the Sermon on the Mount.

> Blessed are the poor in spirit, for theirs is the kingdom of heaven.
> - Matthew 5:3

A man must enter heaven as a pauper, a baby, a poor sinner. Wealth has no value in the kingdom. A person trying to enter in because of wealth or along with his wealth will not be able to.

Job, Abraham, David, as well as Solomon were rich men. Matthew was rich. Lydia was rich. These people were rich, but they were also faithful.

Being rich and successful doesn't stop you from being part of the kingdom, but it can be a dangerous obstacle if you place it before the kingdom. Very few can be both very rich and very spiritual because what creates one wars against the other.

Peter and the Apostles were having trouble with this because, like most Jews of those days, they believed that being wealthy was a sign that God was pleased with you. Your wealth was a sign of God's favor on you. Jesus clarifies this idea and reassures that with faith men can be saved. The Apostles' question was, "If the wealthy (who are favored by God) are in danger of losing their salvation, what chance do poor people like us have?"

Jesus tells them that with or without money, men do not have the ability to save themselves, only God can do this and He does it based on faith, not money. This approach levels the playing field.

> [27] Then Peter said to Him, "Behold, we have left everything and followed You; what then will there be for us?" [28] And Jesus said to them, "Truly I say to you, that you who have followed Me, in the regeneration when the Son of Man will sit on His glorious throne, you also shall sit upon twelve thrones, judging the twelve tribes of Israel. [29] And everyone who has left houses or brothers or sisters or father or mother or children or farms for My name's sake, will receive many times as much, and will inherit eternal life. [30] But many who are first will be last; and the last, first."
> - Matthew 19:27-30

Peter follows up the previous discussion with a question based on what he had heard and seen with Jesus and the rich young ruler. "This fellow had chosen not to follow you, and yet left with his money, prestige and wealthy lifestyle intact. We, on the other hand, have left everything to follow you; where is our reward?" Peter is speaking the mind of the others in saying that they had made the right choice, but unlike the wealthy ruler, they were still poor and rejected.

Jesus' answer describes for the first time the blessings that the King will bestow on those who enter the kingdom by faith:

1. In the kingdom they will be at the seat of authority with God. Judging the twelve tribes was the highest authority and power position they could imagine.

2. Jesus lists the blessings of the here and now (family and possessions) but in the kingdom, the blessings will be of a better kind: peace, righteousness, freedom from the fear of death, fellowship of the saints, etc.

3. Those in the kingdom can look forward to resurrection and eternal life in heaven.

Jesus' final statement summarizes the situation in the present and future:

- Some who are first now (wealth, position, person) will be of no consequence at the judgment because they are missing what is important: faith in Christ.

- Some who are last now (poor, ordinary, powerless) will be first in rank when Jesus comes (seated with Christ on the heavenly throne) because of what they have found and kept here: faith in Jesus Christ.

Lack of faith leads to one person's loss of the kingdom, another's belief brings rewards beyond expectations.

CHAPTER 10
THE KING'S HOUSE

MATTHEW 21:1-23:39

In the last section studied, we read about Jesus' final trip from His home in the northern part of Israel. As He journeys towards Jerusalem we see Him continue His ministry of teaching and healing as He prepares to enter the city where He will suffer a series of challenges and rejections culminating in His crucifixion.

Jesus and the First Visit to the Temple

For the Jews, the temple was the seat of God's power—God dwelled among them in the form of the temple. It was the center of religious, political, social and commercial life. Your standing at the temple determined your standing within Jewish society. In this hierarchy, Jesus stood at the top of the list as the divine Messiah.

The temple was built to exercise the Jewish religion that, in turn, was created to prepare the people and the world for the

Savior. The Savior was now here and ready to be recognized by His people; however we see that instead of welcoming Him to the place that was rightfully His, the Jews unwittingly rejected, tortured and executed Him. This terrible chain of events begins as Jesus, arriving from the northern country, prepares to enter into Jerusalem and the temple which are His.

The Coming

¹ When they had approached Jerusalem and had come to Bethphage, at the Mount of Olives, then Jesus sent two disciples, ² saying to them, "Go into the village opposite you, and immediately you will find a donkey tied there and a colt with her; untie them and bring them to Me. ³ "If anyone says anything to you, you shall say, 'The Lord has need of them,' and immediately he will send them." ⁴ This took place to fulfill what was spoken through the prophet:

⁵ "SAY TO THE DAUGHTER OF ZION,
'BEHOLD YOUR KING IS COMING TO YOU,
GENTLE, AND MOUNTED ON A DONKEY,
EVEN ON A COLT, THE FOAL OF A BEAST OF BURDEN.'"

⁶ The disciples went and did just as Jesus had instructed them, ⁷ and brought the donkey and the colt, and laid their coats on them; and He sat on the coats. ⁸ Most of the crowd spread their coats in the road, and others were cutting branches from the trees and spreading them in the road.

⁹ The crowds going ahead of Him, and those who followed, were shouting,

"Hosanna to the Son of David;

BLESSED IS HE WHO COMES IN THE NAME OF THE LORD;
Hosanna in the highest!"

[10] When He had entered Jerusalem, all the city was stirred, saying, "Who is this?" [11] And the crowds were saying, "This is the prophet Jesus, from Nazareth in Galilee."
- Matthew 21:1-11

Some are confused with the idea of two animals, a donkey and her foal/colt. Jesus was to enter Jerusalem as the prophet Zechariah spoke long before. The prophet said that unlike human kings and saviors who rode in a victory parade on a horse, God's King and Savior would enter the city in a more humble fashion. He would come in on a colt that had never been ridden, thus demonstrating humility and purity. The second animal (the foal's mother) was brought along to steady and reassure the younger animal.

As in many cases, the people, especially the poor, are thrilled to see Jesus arriving, according to scriptures, to the seat of power. They may have thought that with Jesus in Jerusalem things would change. He would be a new and compassionate leader. Once into the city itself the procession causes a stir among the people and Matthew gives us a short clip of a conversation between the group accompanying the Lord in the procession, and the people in the city itself. Remember that most of Jesus' ministry has been done in the north around Galilee. The people accompanying Him point proudly to the fact that the great prophet is from their part of the country.

This will be the high point in Jesus' ministry to these people. Once He goes into the temple area, His opposition will grow.

The Cleansing

> [12] And Jesus entered the temple and drove out all those who were buying and selling in the temple, and overturned the tables of the money changers and the seats of those who were selling doves. [13] And He said to them, "It is written, 'MY HOUSE SHALL BE CALLED A HOUSE OF PRAYER'; but you are making it a ROBBERS' DEN."
>
> [14] And the blind and the lame came to Him in the temple, and He healed them. [15] But when the chief priests and the scribes saw the wonderful things that He had done, and the children who were shouting in the temple, "Hosanna to the Son of David," they became indignant [16] and said to Him, "Do You hear what these children are saying?" And Jesus said to them, "Yes; have you never read, 'OUT OF THE MOUTH OF INFANTS AND NURSING BABIES YOU HAVE PREPARED PRAISE FOR YOURSELF'?" [17] And He left them and went out of the city to Bethany, and spent the night there.
> - Matthew 21:12-17

It helps to understand what's happening here if we realize the reason Jesus was indignant with there people. Selling animals was permitted because the Law required animal sacrifice. It was also lawful to exchange money because Jewish pilgrims came from all over the world to worship at Jerusalem and so needed their foreign currency exchanged so they could purchase animals for sacrifice and pay the temple tax. The problem was that there was plenty of space outside and near the temple walls to do this trading necessary for the proper functioning of the temple. What the Jewish leaders had permitted, however, was to allow these merchants to eventually set up their animal stalls and money tables within the walls of the temple itself. The temple was surrounded by various courtyards that were allotted to different groups of people. At the time this included priests and Levites, men, women as well as Gentile coverts.

With time the leaders had allowed trade and money changing to go on in the courtyard of the Gentiles. This defiled their only area of worship since they couldn't mix with the Jewish worshipers. This was a form of bigotry and disrespect to them and to God. Jesus chases them out and quotes a passage from Isaiah the prophet where Isaiah spoke of the day when even Gentiles would worship the true God and God's temple would universally become a "house of prayer" for both Jews and Gentiles.

By desecrating their courtyard, the Jews were denying these people their chance to worship properly and frustrating the plans of God for His temple and all of the people who desired to worship Him there. After chasing them out, Jesus heals those who come to Him in faith and He receives the praise offered to Him by children.

Matthew demonstrates that it was not that the King was not received in the temple; He was acknowledged, but by those who were furthest down on the scale of importance: those who were infirmed and children. The leaders, however, did not welcome Him. Those entrusted with the leadership, teaching, and preparation of the people and the temple for His coming refused to accept His credentials even after they witness His miracles within the very walls of the temple itself! They rebuke Him for receiving the praise and honor from the children suggesting that it was improper for a mere "man" to receive such praise reserved for God. Jesus directly quotes Psalm 8:2, where David declares that God's majesty is so evident, even children recognize and proclaim it.

The Cursing

> [18] Now in the morning, when He was returning to the city, He became hungry. [19] Seeing a lone fig tree by the road, He came to it and found nothing on it except leaves only; and He said to it, "No longer shall there ever be any fruit from you." And at once the fig tree withered.
>
> [20] Seeing this, the disciples were amazed and asked, "How did the fig tree wither all at once?" [21] And Jesus answered and said to them, "Truly I say to you, if you have faith and do not doubt, you will not only do what was done to the fig tree, but even if you say to this mountain, 'Be taken up and cast into the sea,' it will happen. [22] And all things you ask in prayer, believing, you will receive.
> - Matthew 21:18-22

The Lord spends the night in Bethany (probably with Mary, Martha and Lazarus) before returning to the city the next day. The scene with the fig tree is a living parable that mirrors what is taking place between Jesus and the nation that will reject Him. Fig trees produce their fruit and then the leaves follow gradually (fruit first, then leaves). Seeing the leaves appear, Jesus fully expects to have fruit from the tree, as there should be. It was the time for fruit but the tree only produced leaves; a promise unfulfilled. Jesus curses the tree (not out of anger or vindictiveness); He simply sends it to its demise with a word (it is not good for anything anyways). The parallel, of course, is that Jesus has come at the right time to save His people, and there are signs that they are ready:

- There is temple worship

- There are teachers teaching the word

- These are all the exterior signs of a religious people

But the fruit that Jesus is looking for from them is the fruit of faith and righteousness and brotherly love—this fruit is not present among the trappings of their external religion. The lesson is that what happens to the fig tree will happen to the nation: it will be destroyed to the point where it will not be able to produce fruit any more. The Apostles are amazed wanting to know how Jesus had done this thing to the tree. His answer is a reassurance that the same power at work to wither the tree will be at work in them for the purpose of the gospel. Their preaching and teaching after He is gone will be met with equally great opposition (a mountain of opposition), and their faith will overcome it.

Jesus and the Second Visit to the Temple – Matthew 21:23-25:46

On the second day, Jesus comes to the temple, but this time He makes a less spectacular entrance. On this second visit the various Jewish leaders are ready for Him, and each take turns disputing His authority or directing His claims. Matthew describes what happens as Jesus alternates between confrontations with the leaders and responses to them in the form of parables spoken to the people. Note how the action flows:

- The various leaders attack Him in some way or another.

- Jesus responds to their attacks directly.

- He then teaches the crowds concerning the attacks, in front of His attackers, in parables to the people so that only the believers understand His comments.

- This drives His antagonists to plot His destruction.

We don't have time to read or to go into detail concerning each encounter and subsequent teaching so I will give you an overview of the different scenes as they happened.

Challenge from priests and elders   Matthew 21:23-27

As He enters the temple area on this second visit and begins to teach the crowds, He is immediately challenged by some priests and elders (probably members of the Sanhedrin—ruling council made up of religious leaders). They challenge His legitimacy and His credentials to teach in the temple, an area they controlled. If He claimed His deity, they would stone Him. If He denied His deity, they would dismiss Him. Jesus replies with a question about John the Baptist and what authority he taught by. This put them in a bind because if they acknowledged John's heavenly calling, Jesus would ask them why they didn't obey John. If they dismissed John's authority they would offend and alienate the people and lose their influence. So they refused to answer and Jesus did the same, checkmating their attack.

Parables and teaching for the people - Matthew 21:28-22:14

While the leaders look on:

A. Parable of the two sons – vs. 28-32

After the confrontation, Jesus tells several parables, the first one being a simple story of two sons asked to work by their father. One son says yes but doesn't do it. The other refuses at first, but changes his mind and obeys later on.

Jesus explains that those who disobey and repent will be received by God, and those who give mainly lip service (like these leaders), will be rejected.

B. Parable of the landowner – vs. 33-46

He follows this with the parable of the landowner. In this parable, a landowner leases his land and equipment to others to work. When he sends his people to collect his share at harvest, the workers beat and kill them. Finally, he sends his own son to collect, and they murder him, and because of this the landowner will come to destroy these workers and rent the property out to others who will pay their dues. Jesus goes on to explain that this parable is about the Jews and what will happen to them if they reject God's Son.

In the end Matthew writes that the chief priests and Pharisees were enraged that He spoke against them, and they began a plot to kill Him.

C. Parable of the marriage feast – 22:1-14

Jesus is aware of their intentions and responds with yet another parable, this time one about a marriage feast. In this parable, a king prepares a great feast, but none of the invited guests come, each giving some lame excuse. The king responds by inviting strangers, the poor and the disenfranchised to his meal. The point here is that the Jews were first invited to share the kingdom with Christ, but through their lack of faith, refused. So God had called the non–Jews to share in His kingdom.

Once again, a thinly disguised rebuke of the leaders for their lack of faith and the consequences of this.

Challenge of the Pharisees

> [15] Then the Pharisees went and plotted together how they might trap Him in what He said. [16] And they sent their disciples to Him, along with the Herodians, saying, "Teacher, we know that You are truthful and teach the way of God in truth, and defer to no one; for You are not partial to any. [17] "Tell us then, what do You think? Is it lawful to give a poll-tax to Caesar, or not?" [18] But Jesus perceived their malice, and said, "Why are you testing Me, you hypocrites? [19] "Show Me the coin used for the poll-tax." And they brought Him a denarius. [20] And He said to them, "Whose likeness and inscription is this?" [21] They said to Him, "Caesar's." Then He said to them, "Then render to Caesar the things that are Caesar's; and to God the things that are God's." [22] And hearing this, they were amazed, and leaving Him, they went away.
> - Matthew 22:15-22

The dilemma here was that if Jesus said "Yes, it's ok to pay," they would have denounced Him as a pagan sympathizer. If he said "No," they would accuse Him of stirring up rebellion.

Jesus answers with the essential truth of the matter: do your duty in the human realm, do your duty in the spiritual realm. And with this answer, He silences His attackers.

Challenge of the Sadducees
Matthew 22:23-33

The Sadducees were priests, but priest who came from the upper-class wealthy and noble families. They only held the first five books of the Law to be authoritative and did not believe in the prophets, angels or resurrection. They challenge Him with a riddle about a woman with seven husbands and ask Him whose wife will she be of the seven when she dies and goes to heaven. This was meant to ridicule the idea of an afterlife and heaven. Jesus answers by using a passage from Exodus (one of the books they considered authoritative), and not only solves the riddle but also demonstrates that both the afterlife and heaven are spoken of even in the Pentateuch (the first five books).

This silences and ridicules the Sadducees to the delight of the people.

Challenge of the Pharisees
Matthew 22:34-46

One final time, the leaders come to Jesus with a tricky question. There will be other challenges, but these will come later when He is arrested. The Pharisees, seeing that the Sadducees have been silenced, come to Jesus asking which commandment is greatest in the Law. Now there was a lot of issues hidden in this question:

- Sadducees and Pharisees disagreed on what was important in the scriptures.

- Sadducees only referred to the first five books.

- Pharisees accepted both Law and prophets.

- In addition to this, they created 613 commands (248 positive/365 negative) as a protective shield around the scriptures.

- Another unusual thing they did was to assign numerical value to the Hebrew letters in these commands.

- When one rule came into conflict with another rule, they would weight the value of the rule by the numerical value it contained.

So their question had two proposes: they wanted to further embarrass their religious rivals, the Sadducees, by getting Jesus to side with them; and they wanted Jesus' opinion on a matter (which Law had the highest value) that they debated over endlessly. Jesus answered by going to the heart of the matter: citing the love of God and love of one's fellow man as self as the greatest commands. This was not based on rivalry or formula but on a true summary of all the teaching in the Old Testament.

It was so undeniably true that the Pharisees did not answer or respond negatively. Jesus continues however by posing them a question from a part of scripture they claimed to believe: the Psalms.

The question is one they cannot answer because it can only be discerned through faith in Him, something they didn't have.

The Final Rebuke – Matthew 23:1-39

In this chapter, Jesus will deliver a stinging rebuke directly to the leaders and teachers of the Jews for their failure to prepare the people for His coming.

The next chapter contains seven "woes" or accusations, and finishes with Jesus' lament over the coming destruction of the city and temple, which He will describe in the following chapter.

Summary

So we see in our lesson today that the King came to His city, His temple, His people, and they were not ready. They were worse than not ready; they actually confronted and challenged His royal position.

In the end, He refutes their challenges and mourns the loss of their opportunity to become the true temples of God, in Christ.

CHAPTER 11
THE KING'S JUDGMENT

MATTHEW 24-25

We are studying Matthew's description of Jesus where he emphasizes the royal character of the Lord. All of our lessons have followed this theme of Jesus as the King bringing His heavenly kingdom to those who would receive it here on earth. So far Jesus has demonstrated His royal position:

- By the worship He received as a baby.

- By the witness He has received from the Father, the Holy Spirit and John the Baptist.

- He has demonstrated His exalted position by defeating evil spirits beginning with Satan himself in the desert.

- He has shown Himself to be Lord over disease, infirmity and even death itself with His miracles.

- More recently we have seen His power over the material world with the multiplication of fish and bread, and the calming of a storm.

In the previous chapter we saw Him enter the city of Jerusalem as its King and doing so as the prophets said He would: on the back of a foal, to the joy of the people, the poor, the ill and the outcast. We also noted that the leaders in Jerusalem (Sadducees, Pharisees, priests and elders) challenged Jesus' authority and ministry. It was interesting to see how the Lord responded to every one of their challenges. The end result was that this group was silenced and on some occasions ridiculed, but none of them came to faith—even when their questions and doubts were answered. How many people do we know like this? You answer all their questions, give a good witness, but they still refuse to believe and obey the Lord because they love disbelief more, because disbelief allows them to continue in sin without guilt or fear.

Anyways, once the Lord has finished dealing with the leaders who have rejected Him as the Messiah, He pronounces several woes or judgments upon them because of their disbelief and hypocrisy. After this pronunciation, Jesus and His disciples, who are still in the temple area, begin a discussion about the judgment on the Jews and the end of the world. This takes place as one of the Apostles makes a comment about the temple building itself and Jesus uses the occasion to describe several scenes of judgment. This is why this chapter is entitled, "The King's Judgment."

Jesus is leaving the temple area, and as He leaves the Apostles point out the magnificent buildings of the temple which He has just said will one day be deserted. During that period the temple had undergone fifty years of reconstruction work—the latest effort being paid for by Herod himself. In verses 1-2 Jesus responds to their comments by saying that the buildings will not only be empty, they will be torn down. This sets up further questions by the Apostles (Peter, James,

John, Andrew in Matthew 13:3) who wanted more information about what He has just said. They questioned Him about two things:

- When will the destruction of the temple be?
- What signs will accompany the end of the world that will be brought on by the second coming?

Now, whether the Apostles thought these two events would happen at the same time or at different times, we do not know. We do know from their question, however, that they were asking about two different events.

- The destruction of the temple.
- The return of the Lord and the end of the world.

The following section in Matthew can become confusing so it helps if we divide it into the three views of history that Jesus spoke about in answering His Apostles.

1. Panoramic view – vs. 4-14

In these verses Jesus describes an overview or panoramic view of world history that includes the times before the destruction of the temple, the time after the destruction and the period at the end of time when He will return.

2. Telescope to Jerusalem view – vs. 15-35

In these verses, Jesus telescopes or focuses on one great event in the history of man: the destruction of Jerusalem, which we know took place in 70 AD. Jesus spoke when He was 33, so this event was to take place more than three decades later.

3. Telescope to the second coming - vs. 36-44

Jesus finishes with a look to the far future when He will return ushering in the end of days and the judgment. If we keep these three views in mind, it will help us to untangle these complex verses.

Panorama Until Second Coming

> [4] And Jesus answered and said to them, "See to it that no one misleads you.

This instruction is given so that they will know and avoid false teachers and prophets in these matters.

> [5] For many will come in My name, saying, 'I am the Christ,' and will mislead many. [6] You will be hearing of wars and rumors of wars. See that you are not frightened, for those things must take place, but that is not yet the end. [7] For nation will rise against nation, and kingdom against kingdom, and in various places there will be famines and earthquakes. [8] But all these things are merely the beginning of birth pangs.

The cycle of false prophets, wars and troubles in the world will continue until the end, but these in themselves are not the signs; they are only the beginning of things which will get progressively worse before not only the end of Jerusalem comes, but also the end of the world comes.

> [9] "Then they will deliver you to tribulation, and will kill you, and you will be hated by all nations because of My name. [10] At that time many will fall away and will betray one another and hate one another. [11] Many false prophets will arise and will mislead many. [12] Because

lawlessness is increased, most people's love will grow cold.

This section is parallel to II Thessalonians where Paul talks about the end of the world and what must take place first.

- Apostasy (falling away, love grows cold).
- Man of lawlessness who deceives many through false signs and tries to take the place of God, he will be revealed.
- Jesus describes the devolution of the world (cycle of evil and revival to the end).

¹³ But the one who endures to the end, he will be saved.

In contrast to this, Jesus promises that the faithful will be saved despite these things.

¹⁴ This gospel of the kingdom shall be preached in the whole world as a testimony to all the nations, and then the end will come.

He also promises that the great commission will be carried out and must be carried out before the end can/will come.

This is a panoramic view of the events and flow of history that will occur until His second coming.

Telescope to Fall of Jerusalem

Judea was a rebellious nation and longed to return to the glory days of independence and power enjoyed at the time of Solomon. In the early 60s, they had such unrest that Rome sent troops to this area in order to quell the rebellion. From 66-70 AD the Roman armies successfully laid siege to Jerusalem and totally destroyed the city and temple along with over one million people. This total destruction of the Jewish nation was the fulfillment of Jesus' prophecy to the disciples 33 years earlier described in this passage. The disciples wanted to know when this would happen and Jesus gives them the "signs" to watch out for because many of them would still be alive when it would happen.

> [15] "Therefore when you see the abomination of desolation which was spoken of through Daniel the prophet, standing in the holy place (let the reader understand), [16] then those who are in Judea must flee to the mountains. [17] Whoever is on the housetop must not go down to get the things out that are in his house. [18] Whoever is in the field must not turn back to get his cloak.

The first sign was the "Abomination of Desolation." The point was that when the temple would be desecrated, this would be a sign that destruction was near and they should escape the city.

Daniel (11:31, 12:11) had prophesied that the temple would be defiled and this prophecy was fulfilled in the days of the Maccabees (167-160 BC) by the Syrian King Epiphanes who sacrificed a pig on the altar of the temple. Jesus picks up this idea and says that in the same way, when the temple will be defiled during their lifetime, it will be the signal to escape.

> [20] "But when you see Jerusalem surrounded by armies, then recognize that her desolation is near.

Luke 21:20 tells us that the surrounding of the temple by foreign armies is what constituted defilement. The standards (shields) of the Roman army were idolatrous and often used for worship by the soldiers, and surrounding the temple with these would desecrate it.

Many scholars differ here as to what the abomination is and refer to Jewish historians for events that occurred before, during or after the siege that could fit, but Luke 21:20 is the only biblical reference that refers to this event in context. "He who reads" means he who reads Daniel. Those who read the prophet Daniel along with Christ's cryptogram will be able to know when it's time to get out. Historically we know that many did. In 68 AD the majority of Christians living in Jerusalem escaped to Pella (northwest of Jerusalem in the Decapolis region near the Jordan River) thus avoiding being killed in the massacre.

> [19] But woe to those who are pregnant and to those who are nursing babies in those days! [20] But pray that your flight will not be in the winter, or on a Sabbath. [21] For then there will be a great tribulation, such as has not occurred since the beginning of the world until now, nor ever will.

The tribulation is the suffering caused by the Romans that wiped out the nation.

- Over 1 million killed.

- The combination of the gravity of the sin (Jews who received the blessings and promises but killed their Messiah) and the horror of the punishment (nation wiped out) has not been equaled.

> [22] Unless those days had been cut short, no life would have been saved; but for the sake of the elect those days will be cut short.

God's providence permitted this war to end so that the Christians would not also be annihilated along with the Jews. Their city was destroyed and Romans made no distinction between Christian and non-Christian Jews.

> [23] Then if anyone says to you, 'Behold, here is the Christ,' or 'There He is,' do not believe him. [24] For false Christs and false prophets will arise and will show great signs and wonders, so as to mislead, if possible, even the elect. [25] Behold, I have told you in advance. [26] So if they say to you, 'Behold, He is in the wilderness,' do not go out, or, 'Behold, He is in the inner rooms,' do not believe them.

The believers would naturally associate the destruction of Jerusalem with the return of Jesus, so the Lord warns them against being deceived by those who would claim to be the Lord or speak from God.

- Josephus, Jewish historian of the time, documents how during this period rumors of the Messiah coming or being present circulated in order to keep people in the city.

- In those days, hysteria and fear produced many "prophets" who claimed visions and messages from God.

One false prophet said that he would separate the Sea of Galilee and 25,000 people followed him.

> [27] For just as the lightning comes from the east and flashes even to the west, so will the coming of the Son of Man be.

He tells them that when He does return, it will be evident to all, like lightening across the sky, all will easily and readily know that it is He.

> [28] Wherever the corpse is, there the vultures will gather.

The corpse is the Jewish nation; the vultures are the false Christs and prophets. When you see them in abundance, this will be a second sign that the end of Jerusalem is near.

> [29] "But immediately after the tribulation of those days the sun will be darkened, and the moon will not give its light, and the stars will fall from the sky, and the powers of the heavens will be shaken.

The first word in this verse presents a problem to some: immediately. If we make this next section a discussion about the end of the world and the second coming of Jesus, then it must occur right after the destruction of Jerusalem (some believe and teach Jesus has already returned: 70 AD theory). Since the Man of Lawlessness had not been revealed, Jesus has not returned, therefore this passage must still be talking about events surrounding the destruction of Jerusalem.

> [30] And then the sign of the Son of Man will appear in the sky, and then all the tribes of the earth will mourn, and they will see the Son of Man coming on the clouds of the sky with power and great glory. [31] And He will send forth His angels with a great trumpet and they will gather together His elect from the four winds, from one end of the sky to the other.

Therefore verses 29-31 speak about the destruction and the effects that it has on others and believers. The language is Apocalyptic and is used by prophets to describe cataclysmic historical and political events (Isaiah 13 described the destruction of Babylon in similar language). Language using the symbolism of the destruction of heavenly bodies is used to described the very real fate of the world or the end (II Peter 3:10), but also the end and destruction of a particular nation on the earth. In this case, the end of the Jewish nation as a people under God's special care. The coming of the Son of Man refers to both the second coming at the end of the world and the final judgment, but also any judgment God makes on a particular nation, in this case the nation of Israel.

- It also fits the context of this passage.

- The Jews who rejected Him now will see Him coming as a form of judgment on their nation, a terrible catastrophe that would horrify the world but liberate Christians and the gospel from Jewish persecution.

The Greek word translated "angel" can also be translated as "messenger." This verse can be seen as prophecy concerning the spreading of the gospel throughout the world after the fall of Jerusalem. Verse 14 said this needed to be done before Christ returned, and now with the ideological and cultural restraints of Jerusalem removed, Christianity would flourish even more.

> [32] "Now learn the parable from the fig tree: when its branch has already become tender and puts forth its leaves, you know that summer is near; [33] so, you too, when you see all these things, recognize that He is near, right at the door. [34] Truly I say to you, this generation will not pass away until all these things take place. [35] Heaven and earth will pass away, but My words will not pass away.

Jesus warns them to pay attention to the signs He has given them because they will happen in their generation and He promises by His word that they will happen!

Telescope to Second Coming

Jesus has just explained to them the signs that will preview the destruction of Jerusalem.

1. Preaching of the gospel to all nations (Romans 10:18)
2. Multiplication of false Christs (Josephus)
3. Abomination of the temple (Luke 21:20)
4. Great tribulation (Josephus)

Now in verse 36-44 He makes a contrast using this event with the second coming at the end of the world.

> [36] "But of that day and hour no one knows, not even the angels of heaven, nor the Son, but the Father alone.

No one knows the time. Not even Jesus while He is with His disciples. This refers to His second coming, not the destruction of Jerusalem in 70 AD.

> [37] For the coming of the Son of Man will be just like the days of Noah. [38] For as in those days before the flood they were eating and drinking, marrying and giving in marriage, until the day that Noah entered the ark, [39] and they did not understand until the flood came and took them all away; so will the coming of the Son of Man be.

There will be no cataclysmic signs and all will seem normal. Normal in the sense that the believers will be preparing themselves for the second coming and the end of the world, while the rest of the world will be ignoring it until it will be too late (just like in the time of Noah).

> [40] Then there will be two men in the field; one will be

taken and one will be left. [41] Two women will be grinding at the mill; one will be taken and one will be left.

Some take this verse to mean that before Jesus returns some will be taken in a "rapture" and disappear to be with God in heaven. This is part of the Pre-Millennialist view of the rapture and 1000-year sign. In context, however, Jesus is talking about readiness and He says that when He returns suddenly one will be saved, one lost; no time for repentance and change. Just like Noah, when the rain came, they were taken and disappeared into the ark; the others remained outside to die in the flood.

When Jesus comes, the faithful will be taken to be with Him and the disbelievers immediately put away from His promise.

[42] "Therefore be on the alert, for you do not know which day your Lord is coming. [43] But be sure of this, that if the head of the house had known at what time of the night the thief was coming, he would have been on the alert and would not have allowed his house to be broken into. [44] For this reason you also must be ready; for the Son of Man is coming at an hour when you do not think He will.

Since the end is to be like this, we should always be prepared and not foolishly lapse into sin, thinking we have plenty of time to repent and be ready for the return; we now know, and thus we must be ready.

Exhortation to Vigilance 24:45-25:30

After responding to the question of the judgment on Jerusalem and His return, Jesus warns them to be vigilant and does so with these parables:

1. Parable of the evil slave – 24:45-51

Here the lesson is not to presume we have the luxury of sinning because the end is far away, it can come at any time and the judgment is sure for those who are unfaithful.

2. Parable of the 10 virgins – 25:1-13

Here Jesus warns against the foolishness of not being ready, not a question of gross evil, but rather negligence. To neglect Christ will bring destruction in the end as will.

3. Parable of the talents – 25:14-30

Here the warning is for those who are in the kingdom but who fail to expand its borders, fail to serve the King with zeal. This slave was not caught or surprised unprepared, he just assumed that his preparation was sufficient when it wasn't.

All these parables have the element of preparation, judgment and punishment for those who neglect to prepare for the return of the Master.

Judgment Scene – 25:31-46

The climax of the discourse is the judgment scene at the end of the world. Those found to be righteous have obeyed the commands to love God (refer to Him as Lord) as well as their neighbor; this was the way to prepare. Those condemned have the same judgment and are condemned because they did not love their neighbor.

The punishment and reward is eternal in nature. The overarching theme is: be ready.

CHAPTER 12
THE KING'S VICTORY

MATTHEW 28:1-20

Let's wrap up our study by reviewing Matthew's final chapters where Jesus the King wins His great victory over death, and turns authority over to His Apostles. Previously we examined Jesus' prophesy about the eventual destruction that Jerusalem would suffer because of the Jewish peoples' rejection of Him as the Messiah, as well as a prophecy concerning His eventual return at the end of the world to judge mankind. Of course, these prophecies might have sounded a little far-fetched at that moment, but His words would grow in importance once the resurrection was completed.

The Passion in Matthew

Many writers and commenters have referred to the last hours of Jesus' life, including His torture and crucifixion, as the Passion. And so, like the other three gospel writers, Matthew devotes the final portion of his written word to the Passion and resurrection of Jesus, and like Mark, adds the commission Jesus gave to the Apostles. The Passion is divided into three sections:

1. The final hours with the Apostles – 26:1-56

The time with the Apostles included several scenes:

The anointing

A woman anoints Jesus' head with costly perfume. This was a gesture of honor and respect prefiguring His death as His body was being prepared for the grave. This was done as Jesus ate with the disciples at the home of Simon, a leper who lived in Bethany. Matthew explains that it was at this moment that Judas decided to make an arrangement with the Jewish leaders to betray Jesus.

The Lord's Supper

It was the time of the Passover when thousands of Jews from all over the world converged on Jerusalem to observe this religious feast. They would offer a lamb as sacrifice and gather together to eat the Passover meal in remembrance of the time when they were liberated from Egyptian slavery many years before. Jesus, a good Jew, gathered His Apostles and together they shared the Passover meal. Near the end of the meal however, Jesus instituted a new "meal" of sorts. He told His disciples that from that day forward they would share the Lord's Supper of bread and wine in order to commemorate His death on the cross. There was to be no more sacrificing of the lamb because He was the final sacrifice for sin. He was to be the Lamb of God. There was to be no more bitter herbs to eat as a reminder of their bitter experience of slavery. From now on the unleavened bread would represent His pure and broken body on the cross, and the fruit of the vine/wine would represent His blood shed for sin. The entire experience would now commemorate their freedom from sin to a promise of an eternal home in heaven with God, obtained by His sacrificial death on the cross as payment for the sins of all humanity.

Gethsemane

The third event with the Apostles takes place in a garden outside the city walls of Jerusalem. At this place Jesus struggles with His human nature, which is recoiling at the thought of what He will have to face. This would be a natural reaction for the human part of His nature to have. In the end, the Apostles are with Him, but not much help because they are weary with sorrow and sleep. The final scene shows the Lord coming to grips with the horror before Him, and as He does, Judas the traitor arrives to betray Him into the hands of the Jewish authorities. At this point the Apostles scatter just as Jesus said they would.

What is interesting about these events is that each one continues a prophetic element about the death to come: the anointing for burial, the supper of remembrance, the garden of suffering and surrender.

Note that in each instance the Lord is preparing Himself and His Apostles for the death He will endure.

2. The trials

Jesus had several trials or hearings that were organized in unlawful ways. Contrary to the Law, they were done at night and were convened without all the leaders present. Of course, the purpose was not to determine truth, these show trials were conducted to provide a reason and charge for which He could be executed. Matthew describes the scenes:

The trial before Caiaphas

Caiaphas was the high priest at that time, and Jesus was first brought to him from the garden after the betrayal by Judas. Here He is mocked and baited by those assembled. They have no charge as one accuser after another contradicts himself. Finally, out of exasperation, Caiaphas asks Jesus directly if He thinks He is the Messiah. Jesus does not deny the claim and in so doing gives Caiaphas the charge he so desperately is looking for: blasphemy. Under Jewish Law blasphemy was punishable by death, but while they were under Roman rule the Jews did not have the civil and legal authority to carry out the death penalty. This could only be decreed by a Roman court and carried out by Roman law.

The trial before Pilate

The Jews now bring Jesus before Pilate hoping to persuade him to carry out the death penalty they have levied on Jesus. Pilate, in examining Jesus, finds nothing under Roman law to justify the execution of this man. On the contrary, the more he speaks with Jesus, the more he wants to release Him. Even Pilate's wife appeals to her husband to let the Jewish prisoner go, having had a dream of Him.

Pilate then tries to exchange Jesus for a notorious murderer, but to no avail. The Jews are adamant. Finally, when Pilate sees that the Jewish leaders are fomenting a riot over the issue, he relents and permits the execution to go forward. The release of one innocent Jew was not worth the trouble a riot would cause on his watch.

In both trials, no proof or credible charge was made, no guilt was found, no crime was committed and no justice meted out. Jesus was falsely accused, illegally tried, improperly sentenced and brutally executed for being who He really was!

3. The crucifixion and burial – 27:57-66

Matthew continues to describe the Passion in the third section of this narrative by relating the events of Jesus' crucifixion and burial.

Crucifixion

Roman crucifixion was merciless, excruciating and deadly, so much so that a Roman citizen was not allowed to be put to death in this way. It was reserved for the worst criminals, slaves and foreigners. Matthew does not provide much detail about the crucifixion itself, but does describe the reaction of the people who were present at the cross:

- The soldiers gambled for His clothing.

- The crowd mocked His helplessness.

- The Jewish leaders taunted Him.

- The criminals crucified at His side derided Him.

Matthew also describes the unusual things that took place once Jesus actually died:

- The veil of the temple was torn.

- The earth shook.

- Some were raised from the dead who had been disciples and believers.

- One of the centurions who had participated in the crucifixion was converted on the spot.

Matthew also describes the fact that the Romans placed a sign above His head that read, "This is Jesus, the king of the Jews." The Romans had put it there to annoy and humiliate the Jewish leaders. They had objected and wanted Pilate to write, "He said, I am the king of the Jews" (John 19:21) thus humiliating Jesus and not themselves. Pilate, however, was adamant, and the sign remained as it was originally written. Despite the lies and disbelief, what was written above the head of the Lord, as a form of mockery, was the exact truth of the matter.

The Jews, in collaboration with the Roman authorities, had executed their own Messiah and, to make matters worse, had done it through the hand of pagan Rome.

The Burial

Matthew goes on to describe the scene as Joseph of Arimathea and Mary Magdalene prepare the body for burial. There were others who participated, but Matthew mentions only these two. He also describes how the Jews, knowing of Jesus' prophecies concerning His resurrection, go to Pilate to make sure the tomb is properly guarded. Pilate permits them to double the guard and put a seal on the stone so there would be no tampering or switching of bodies.

This is the final scene leading up to the glorious event where Jesus will provide insurmountable proof to confirm His claim as King of the kingdom of God in heaven as well as King of the kingdom of God on earth.

The Resurrection – 28:1-15

> [1] Now after the Sabbath, as it began to dawn toward the first day of the week, Mary Magdalene and the other Mary came to look at the grave.

It was early Sunday morning as several of His female disciples come with the hope of finishing the burial procedure left undone because Jesus' death occurred too near the Sabbath day.

> [2] And behold, a severe earthquake had occurred, for an angel of the Lord descended from heaven and came and rolled away the stone and sat upon it. [3] And his appearance was like lightning, and his clothing as white as snow. [4] The guards shook for fear of him and became like dead men.

Matthew describes what happened before the women had arrived that morning. The angel's presence had caused an earthquake when He rolled the stone away. The angel appeared as a man (they always do in the Bible). Matthew describes the angel in terms of bright light (common for spiritual beings to be described this way; i.e. Jesus at transfiguration). The guards fainted (they were afraid and unworthy to see the sight of the risen Christ).

> [5] The angel said to the women, "Do not be afraid; for I know that you are looking for Jesus who has been crucified. [6] He is not here, for He has risen, just as He said. Come, see the place where He was lying. [7] Go quickly and tell His disciples that He has risen from the dead; and behold, He is going ahead of you into Galilee, there you will see Him; behold, I have told you."

The angel instructs the women as to what has happened and what they should do.

> [8] And they left the tomb quickly with fear and great joy and ran to report it to His disciples. [9] And behold, Jesus met them and greeted them. And they came up and took hold of His feet and worshiped Him. [10] Then Jesus said to them, "Do not be afraid; go and take word to My brethren to leave for Galilee, and there they will see Me."

On their way to do this, Jesus appears to them and they worship Him as the King.

He also repeats the instructions of the angel (who originally received them from the Lord).

> [12] And when they had assembled with the elders and consulted together, they gave a large sum of money to the soldiers, [13] and said, "You are to say, 'His disciples came by night and stole Him away while we were asleep.' [14] And if this should come to the governor's ears, we will win him over and keep you out of trouble." [15] And they took the money and did as they had been instructed; and this story was widely spread among the Jews, and is to this day.

Matthew describes the scene where the Jewish leaders construct a story to explain the disappearance of the body and the amazing experience of the soldiers. It is interesting to note that Matthew credits this story as something that was still being spread by the Jews as a way to discredit the resurrection; even some thirty years later when Matthew was writing and circulating this gospel.

But Jesus has risen and the tide of human history will now change forever. A new King is crowned to rule over the kingdom that God has established on the earth in place of the evil ruler that held the power of death over the people.

One royal duty remains for the King to carry out.

The Commission – 28:16-20

Jesus' position as the Savior/King has been established fulfilling all the prophecies about Him. The prophets said that the Messiah and true King of God's people would provide proof of His identity by resurrecting from the dead. Many prophets and leaders did miracles, raised the dead and won great victories, but only the Messiah/King would die for the people and resurrect three days later. This was the final proof of His identity as King/Savior "who was declared the Son of God with power by the resurrection from the dead" Romans 1:4.

Now that this fact has been established, there remains one last act for the King to do. He now gives His Apostles a commission and the authority to proclaim the King's message throughout the world. The commission and message are the following:

> [18] And Jesus came up and spoke to them, saying, "All authority has been given to Me in heaven and on earth. [19] Go therefore and make disciples of all the nations, baptizing them in the name of the Father and the Son and the Holy Spirit, [20] teaching them to observe all that I commanded you; and lo, I am with you always, even to the end of the age."

1. He gives them the authority to speak with authority.

2. They are to proclaim His rule as King and His offer of salvation as Messiah.
3. They are to proclaim the way into the kingdom (faith and obedience).
4. He promises to be with them until the end (which He has already talked about in Matthew 24-25, the end of Jerusalem for them/the end of the world for all other disciples).

This is the message we are charged with today.

- He is our King.
- This is our authority.
- The gospel is our message to proclaim.
- He will be with us in this work until we die or He returns, whichever comes first.

Grace and honor be to our King and Savior, Jesus Christ, forever and forever, Amen.

More from BibleTalk Books

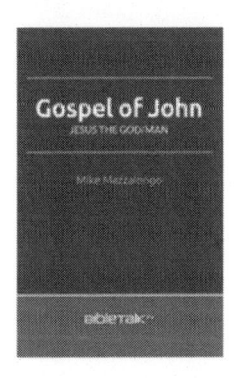

- Christianity for Beginners
- Colossians for Beginners
- Daniel / Revelation for Beginners
- In Spirit and In Truth: The Fundamentals of Biblical Worship
- Gospel of John: Jesus the God/Man
- Jude for Beginners
- In Love for Life: Building or Rebuilding a Great Marriage
- The Kingdom Parables
- Life of Jesus in Chronological Order

BibleTalk.tv is an Internet Mission Work.

We provide textual Bible teaching material on our website and mobile apps for free. We enable churches and individuals all over the world to have access to high quality Bible materials for personal growth, group study or for teaching in their classes.

The goal of this mission work is to spread the gospel to the greatest number of people using the latest technology available. For the first time in history it is becoming possible to preach the gospel to the entire world at once. BibleTalk.tv is an effort to preach the gospel to all nations every day until Jesus returns.

The Choctaw Church of Christ in Oklahoma City is the sponsoring congregation for this work and provides the oversight for the BibleTalk ministry team. If you would like information on how you can support this ministry, please go to the link provided below.

---

bibletalk.tv/support

Made in the USA
Lexington, KY
17 November 2019